The Role of Japan in Asia

Shinichi Ichimura

An International Center for Economic Growth Publication

 **PRESS**

San Francisco, California

Publication signifies that the International Center for Economic Growth believes a work to be a competent treatment worthy of public consideration. The findings, interpretations, and conclusions of a work are entirely those of the authors and should not be attributed to ICEG, its affiliated organizations, its Board of Overseers, or organizations that support ICEG.

Publication of this Occasional Paper was funded by the United States Agency for International Development (AID).

Inquiries, book orders, and catalog requests should be addressed to ICS Press, 720 Market Street, San Francisco, California 94102, USA. Telephone: (415) 981-5353; fax: (415) 986-4878; book orders within the contiguous United States: **(800) 326-0263.**

Library of Congress Cataloging-in-Publication Data

Ichimura, Shin 'ichi, 1925–
    The role of Japan in Asia / Shinichi Ichimura.
        p.   cm. — (Occasional papers ; 36)
    Includes bibliographical references.
    ISBN 1-55815-242-3
    1. Japan—Economic conditions—1945- 2. Asia—Economic conditions—1945- I. Title. II. Series: Occasional papers (International Center for Economic Growth) ; no. 36.
    HC462.9.I333 1993
    338.952—dc20   92-46607
                                                                CIP

CONTENTS

PREFACE

The International Center for Economic Growth is pleased to publish *The Role of Japan in Asia* as the thirty-sixth in our series of Occasional Papers, which present reflections on broad policy issues by noted scholars and policy makers. This monograph brings together two essays by Dr. Shinichi Ichimura, distinguished director of the Institute of International Relations at Osaka International University.

In the first, and more comprehensive, essay, the author examines the transformation of Japan from a resource-poor, poverty-stricken, occupied country to the economic superpower it is today. He shows that Japan's success has contributed in several ways to wider economic development in Asia: through trade, through direct investment abroad, through official and private lending, through technology transfer, through transfers of human resources and information (including Japanese-style business management), and through rapidly expanding official development assistance. Dr. Ichimura offers recommendations for actions Japan can take in the future to sustain and encourage development in Asia. In the shorter essay that concludes this work, the author concentrates on the role of education and of technological development in promoting economic growth, presenting Japan's experience as an instructive example for other economies in Asia.

We are confident that Dr. Ichimura's understanding of Asian economic events since World War II and his strong support of increased Japanese international economic cooperation will make his remarks of great interest to scholars and policy makers concerned with well-being in the Asian Pacific economies in particular and in all developing countries.

Nicolás Ardito-Barletta
General Director
International Center for Economic Growth

Panama City, Panama
April 1993

ABOUT THE AUTHOR

Shinichi Ichimura, a Japanese citizen, is vice chancellor of Osaka International University and general director of that university's Institute of International Relations. He joined the newly established university in 1988, after two decades of distinguished service at Kyoto University, where he was professor of economics and director of the Center for Southeast Asian Studies. He has a long-standing interest in Asian development economics and in the comparative study of Pacific economies.

SHINICHI ICHIMURA

Introduction

The two essays that make up this Occasional Paper were written to explain to the international reader the reasons for and the process of Japanese and Asian economic development, particularly in the post–World War II period. The first essay is a paper that was presented at the International Center for Economic Growth's meeting of Asian correspondent institutes in Malaysia in 1990, and the second is a short version of a paper presented at the Korea Institute for Economics and Technology, also in 1990.

Japanese experiences in economic development provide highly instructive lessons for the developing countries of Asia, in both positive and negative ways. Despite Japan's remarkable achievement in economic growth and the impressive rise in the standard of living within a few decades, one should not ignore the unfortunate darker side of Japanese economic development. Regional discrepancies in the economic welfare of the nation, extremely high property prices and rent in major cities, and the symptoms of social deterioration already noticeable in urban living are only a few examples of conditions that are sources of serious concern. Nevertheless, I have not approached those problems in these essays and must ask the reader to await a discussion of them in my forthcoming book *Economic Essays on Japan and Asia*. Until publication of that volume, I shall be happy to make some of my previously published work, such as *Nihon Keizai no Shinro o motomete* (Searching for the course of the Japanese economy), available to interested readers of Japanese who write to me.

1

Contributions of Private Enterprise

The greatest contribution of Japan to Asian development is the country's demonstration of successful economic and political development as a non-Western nation, going in only a few generations from the poverty-stricken feudal conditions of the Edo period to the prosperous modern, or even postindustrial, society of the present. The miraculous reconstruction of a devastated land after World War II and the nation's further development as a global economic power has been more than even the Japanese people themselves expected. This performance was by no means easy, however, because there was no precedent for a country in Asia to learn how to catch up with the West and modernize itself quickly without being colonized—as many other countries in Asia, Central and South America, and Africa were. Many Asian nations could take Japan as an economic precedent, if not a political precedent, and follow the same path of rapid economic development, unlike many other underdeveloped countries in Latin America, Africa, or West Asia.

In order to explain what kind of issues Japan and other Asian countries have faced and how they resolved difficult problems to achieve impressive development in the 1970s and the 1980s, I shall first survey the growth performance and overall pattern of Asian economic development; second, I shall briefly describe the political economy of postwar Japan; and, third, I shall compare the various factors for Japan's and other Asian countries' economic and sociopolitical development. In these discussions particular attention will be paid to relevant economic policies of the Japanese government.

Patterns of Asian Development

The economic performance of Asian countries over the past several decades has surprised everyone in the world. Asia was once known as the place of Oriental despotism and widespread, irreducible poverty.

2

Even as late as 1968 the *Asian Drama* was conceived as a tragedy of stagnation by no less an authority than Dr. Gunnar Myrdal. This pessimism gradually yielded to optimism, however, as most Asian underdeveloped countries began to emulate the fast growth of the Japanese economy, which grew in terms of per capita GNP from US$300 in 1948 to US$12,750 in 1987. Even so, the most authoritative study, known as the Hla Myint report, undertaken by an Asian Development Bank study group just before 1970 and published in 1971, predicted only a modest 5.5 percent growth rate for East and Southeast Asian countries in the 1970s. The actual performance turned out to be 7.4 percent, the East and Southeast Asian countries achieving faster growth than countries in any other region of the world, whether industrialized or developing and including the oil-rich Middle Eastern countries as well. Figure 1 illustrates this rapid rise in GNP per capita for each country in Asia.

These economies, however, have not developed at the same rate or to the same degree. In fact, on the basis of their growth performances, we may classify them into six groups:

1. Japan alone as an industrial market economy—highest in GNP per capita as well as largest in output

2. Singapore, Hong Kong, Taiwan, and South Korea forming a cluster of newly industrializing economies (often referred to as the Asian NIES)

3. Malaysia, Thailand, the Philippines, and Indonesia (the ASEAN countries of Southeast Asia minus Singapore), which we shall refer to as the ASEAN-4

4. China and India, developing countries like the ASEAN-4 but with special characteristics stemming from their enormous size, leading us to identify them as giant economies in Asia

5. the typically agrarian economies in South Asia, namely, Pakistan, Sri Lanka, Nepal, and Myanmar

6. the stagnant socialist economies: three economies in Indochina, and North Korea

FIGURE 1   Performance of Asian Development for 1965–1985

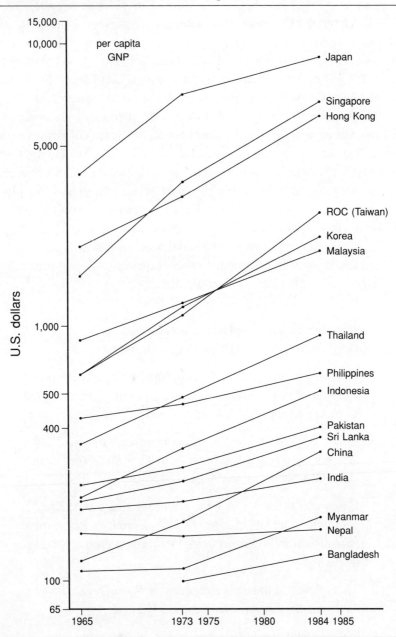

NOTE: Intervals indicated on the Y axis are not constant.

TABLE 1 Grouping of Selected Asian Economies, 1965–1986

	Population (millions)	GNP per capita (1986, dollars)	GDP (billions of dollars)	Growth rate 1965–86 (percentage)	Inflation rate (percentage)	
					1965–80	1981–86
Industrial market economy						
Japan	121.5	12,840	1955.7	4.3	7.8	1.6
NIES						
Singapore	2.6	7,410	17.3	7.6	4.7	1.9
Hong Kong	5.4	6,910	32.3	6.2	8.1	6.9
Taiwan	19.0	3,000	57.0	9.0	9.6	6.2
South Korea	41.5	2,370	98.2	6.7	18.8	5.4
Developing economies						
Malaysia	16.1	1,830	27.6	4.3	4.9	1.4
Thailand	52.6	810	41.8	4.0	6.8	3.0
Philippines	57.3	560	30.5	1.9	11.7	18.2
Indonesia	166.4	490	75.2	4.6	34.3	8.9

(continued on next page)

TABLE 1 (continued)

	Population (millions)	GNP per capita (1986, dollars)	GDP (billions of dollars)	Growth rate 1965–86 (percentage)	Inflation rate (percentage)	
					1965–80	1981–86
Giant economies						
China	1054.0	300	271.9	5.1	0.0	3.8
India	781.4	290	203.8	1.8	4.6	6.0
South Asia						
Sri Lanka	16.1	400	5.9	2.9	9.6	13.5
Pakistan	99.2	350	30.1	2.4	10.3	7.5
Myanmar	38.0	200	8.2	2.3	8.7	2.1
Bangladesh	103.2	160	15.5	0.4	14.9	11.2
Nepal	17.0	141	2.2	1.9	7.7	8.8

SOURCES: World Development Report 1988; National Statistical Yearbooks; Asian Development Bank, Key Indicators of Developing Member Countries of ADB (July 1989).

If we group Japan and the NIES together, these groupings correspond in a general way to the resource endowments characteristic of each group: Japan and the NIES being poor in natural resources, the ASEAN-4 being relatively rich in natural resources, and China and India being advantageously endowed with both. Given the different circumstances these states found themselves in, therefore, it would be surprising indeed if the same growth strategy had been adopted by all. Thus, it would seem that the development strategies of the Japanese economy may not have direct relevance to those of the other two groups, except in the immediate postwar period or for certain aspects of the industrialization policies in the later stages of other Asian economies' development.

The resource-poor economies (Japan and the NIES) have pursued a strategy designed to overcome their weakness in natural resources and take advantage of their human capital. The first step in this strategy was to develop labor-intensive light industries such as textiles and footwear and then to increase productivity and export the products. The next step was to use the foreign exchange earned in this way to import capital equipment to invest in infrastructure and in these and additional export industries. Exports were further expanded and higher levels of industrialization were attained. Government support in the form of various subsidies usually plays a crucial role in the early stage of industrialization.

The resource-rich economies (the ASEAN-4) pursued a different strategy, centering on the exploitation of the natural resources which they had in abundance. The first step in this strategy was to explore for oil and other mineral resources or to develop primary (agricultural, fishery, and forestry) industries. These natural resources, primary products, and processed raw materials were then exported, the foreign exchange earnings being used to pay for imported capital goods, which were invested in infrastructure and resource exploration, agro-industry, resource-related industries, or, if government desired, light industries. Countries following this model usually require a significant amout of investment in human capital, because they are the countries seriously short of skilled workers, engineers, bureaucrats, and businessmen. Only after a preparatory stage of development does a gradual shift to a higher degree of industrialization become possible.

Giant economies (China and India), as countries rich in both human and natural resources, did not feel forced to follow exclusively either

TABLE 2   Basic Indicators of Development in Asian Economies

	GNP growth rate	GDP growth rate		Industrial growth rate	
	1960s	1965–73	1974–84	1965–73	1974–84
Industrial market economy					
Japan	10.4	9.8	4.3	13.5	5.9
NIES					
Singapore	7.6	13.0	8.2	17.6	8.6
Hong Kong	8.0	7.9	9.8	8.4	8.0
Taiwan	9.2	9.0	10.3	12.0	13.5
South Korea	6.4	10.0	7.2	18.4	11.2
Developing economies					
Malaysia	6.2	6.7	7.3	4.6	8.7
Thailand	6.2	7.8	6.8	9.0	8.7
Philippines	5.9	5.4	4.8	7.4	5.3
Indonesia	3.0	8.1	6.8	13.4	8.3
Giant economies					
China		7.8	6.6	12.1	8.7
India		3.9	4.1	3.7	4.1
South Asia					
Pakistan	2.5	5.4	5.6	6.6	7.6
Sri Lanka		4.2	5.2	7.3	4.8
Myanmar		2.9	6.0	3.6	7.7
Nepal	1.8	1.7	3.1	—	—
Bangladesh	3.3	—	5.0	−6.1	7.6
Socialist economies Vietnam					
North	6.0	—	—	—	—
South	3.6	—	—	—	—
Kampuchea	2.5	2.7	—	—	—
Laos	4.5	—	—	—	—
Korea, North	6.0	—	—	—	—

Blank cell = not applicable; dash = not available.
SOURCES: *World Development Report, 1985–1988*; National Statistical Yearbooks; Asian Development Bank, *Key Indicators of Developing Member Countries of ADB* (July 1989).

of these strategies. Instead, they found it possible to undertake development on several different fronts at the same time. The first step was natural resource exploration and agricultural development. Industrialization was pursued simultaneously for a considerable period utilizing out-of-date technology and without relying much on external trade or foreign investment. Capital was largely squeezed from domestic savings and invested in infrastructure and certain strictly protected, labor-intensive industries. Exports were limited to selected natural resources, primary products, and light industrial products. Imports were restricted to minimum essentials for industrialization. Eventually, of course, this simultaneous effort tended to retard technological progress, so that as the pace of development fell behind that in surrounding industrializing countries of smaller scale, demands were generated for "opening up" the economy.

Since the experiences of Japanese economic development are not directly relevant to the South Asian economies and to the socialist economies in Asia, details of their development will not be discussed in this essay.

Political Economy of Japanese Development, 1945–1988

The growth of the modern Japanese economy was a challenge to the Western world in terms of long-term rate of growth in per capita income before World War II—but more so after the war. This section presents my view of the postwar development of the Japanese economy within its political setting in the world. It is convenient to divide the postwar era of Japan into the following six periods:

1. 1945–1952: the occupation period

2. 1952–1960: the reconstruction period

3. 1960–1970: the rapid growth period

4. 1970–1980: the shocks period

5. 1980–1990: the internationalization period

6. 1990–2000: the trial period

The last two periods cover contemporary times, so their issues will be examined in later sections. Initially, the political economy in the first four periods will be discussed.

The occupation period. This period should be regarded as fundamentally a continuation of wartime, when every initiative was taken by the occupation authorities. Some political analysts characterize the occupation policies in the immediate postwar period as guided by three *D*s: Demilitarization, Democratization, and De-monopolization.

Politically the occupation authorities not only executed and punished the persons whom they regarded as war criminals but also purged all the important political and business leaders and ordered the Japanese government to do what they regarded as necessary to keep Japan from becoming a threat to them again. The accomplishment of their prime objective was symbolized by enacting the new Japanese constitution, whose original version was prepared by a few American officials in the office of the supreme commander for the Allied powers (SCAP) in a few weeks. This constitution restricted the use of Japanese military power strictly to self-defense. All laws and regulations that restricted the freedom of speech, press, and association were abolished, and the constitution recognized women's suffrage.

Economically, the occupation authorities ordered the passage of the Fundamental Labor Law and liberalized the labor union movement. They also ordered implementation of the land reform that had been prepared by the Japanese government in prewar days and dissolved the *zaibatsu*s (big business conglomerates) by passing a law to remove excessive concentration. All these policies had advantages and disadvantages for postwar political and economic development. It cannot be denied that the sudden introduction of liberal democracy to postwar Japan caused a great deal of social unrest for more than a decade. As far as the effects on economic growth are concerned, however, they have been largely favorable for maintaining the competitive character of the Japanese economy up to the present time.

Well before the outbreak of the Korean War in June 1950, indeed as early as 1947, the occupation policies changed from those of the American New Dealers and took a more conservative, anticommunist direction. Many radical labor and student movements were suppressed by the occupation authorities. The Police Reserve Forces were organized as a miniature army. Despite all the confusion in the postwar chaos the reconstruction of the Japanese economy began step by step with the initiatives of new leaders as well as with the help of those who were released from the purge. The war damage in Japan, amounting to one-quarter of national wealth, was more serious than that in Germany. Nevertheless, the Japanese people struggled for survival with the help of generous supplies of foodstuffs from the occupation forces and with sound policy guidance, such as the Dodge plan on fiscal and monetary policies for stability. As a result, the Japanese economic recovery was as impressive as the German reconstruction.

The reconstruction period.   During this period the Japanese nation devoted its total energy, day and night, from the northern corner of Hokkaido to the southern tip of Kyushu (Okinawa was still under occupation), with determination and initiative, to completing as soon as possible reconstruction to the highest prewar standard of living and industrialization. The so-called Jimmu boom (Jimmu was the first emperor in Japanese history) in 1956 gave Japanese businesses the impression that a new postwar era was dawning, going beyond the best prewar record in many industrial indices.

During this period, however, the Japanese government was still concerned with the country's relations with the outside world. The most important goal was to return to the international community after World War II by joining the United Nations as a full member. This was achieved by concluding the USSR–Japan Joint Declaration in 1956 and having the Soviet Union's agreement to admit Japan to the United Nations in 1956. The next concern among Japanese politicians was their dissatisfaction with many of the restrictions imposed during the occupation period. Among the problems, there were two major ones. One was the Japanese constitution, and the other was the Mutual Security Agreement (MSA) between Japan and the United States. The former involved two prime issues from the Japanese point of view. The first was its non-conformity with the historical tradition of the Japanese monarchy, and the second was a too-restrictive article on defense (Article 9). The Mutual

Security Agreement concluded during the occupation period did not oblige the United States to defend Japan in an emergency, despite its right to intervene in Japan's internal affairs in time of crisis. Article 9 and this feature of the MSA made Prime Minister Kishi worry about the security of the Japanese nation. He tried to amend these two elements of occupation policy as well as to reestablishing friendly relations with the United States and Southeast Asian countries. For these purposes he visited Southeast Asia, as the first Japanese prime minister to do so after the war, to start negotiation of reparation payments and also visited the United States to initiate the revision of the Mutual Security Agreement.

In 1960 the new United States–Japan Security Agreement was passed by the Japanese parliament, but only after very serious rioting on the streets around the parliamentary building. Left wing groups, including the Communist party, the Socialist party, the leftist labor union Sohyo, radical student groups, and "progressive intellectuals" were not only genuinely worried about Japan's possible return to its prewar course but also regarded this moment as the best chance to fight back against the conservative trends started in the latter half of the occupation period. Many Communist countries and parties abroad as well as some journalists and university professors at home seemed to support this antigovernment movement—until the last moment. When the demonstrators on the streets appeared to be turning to violence by intruding into the Diet assembly hall and when they revealed their true intent—to negate parliamentary democracy through irresponsible demagoguery—the top editors of the leading newspapers belatedly issued a joint communiqué stating that they did not support violence for political ends and that they abhorred the actions of groups seeking to impose their own views by violence.

When the new MSA was finally passed by the parliament, there occurred two effects. First, most of those journalists, intellectuals, and professors who supported the radical movement announced their "disillusion" or despair, and many of them gradually changed their views on international relations to become pro-Western or pro-American and often strongly anticommunist. Second, the leaders of the Liberal Democratic party were inclined to avoid political confrontation with the opposition parties and radical groups and found it wiser to concentrate on economic affairs and try to raise the standard of living for the common people. This was in a sense a return to the Yoshida doctrine of concentration on economic growth (as promulgated by Prime Minister Yoshida in the very early postwar period).

The period of rapid economic growth. This period was characterized by the Income-doubling Plan of the Ikeda cabinet. Prime Minister Ikeda succeeded Prime Minister Kishi and changed the tone of Japanese politics from one of confrontation to one that adopted a low profile and followed Ikeda's new slogan of "generosity and patience." The new prime minister succeeded in turning the attention of the Japanese people—and the press—from the political struggle among different ideologies to the effort to improve the social welfare among the common people. The political season was over, and the economic season had begun. This was what the citizens of Japan had been awaiting so long, during several decades of perseverance and striving.

In this period Japanese GNP almost quadrupled. From 1955 to 1971 Japanese GNP kept increasing at an annual rate of more than 10 percent. The production index of mining and manufacturing became 8.2 times what it was in 1955; exports became 10 times as much as in 1955; and wages became 3.5 times as much. Japanese GNP became the second highest in the free world, and the country's position in the Western alliance could no longer be ignored. At the same time Prime Minister Ikeda visited Thailand and took a bold step in concluding a reparation agreement with the Thai government. This was the beginning of Japanese economic cooperation with developing countries in the name of reparation payment.

Toward the end of the 1960s some political turbulence occurred again around the United States–Japan Mutual Security Agreement. This agreement had a term of ten years, and left wing radicals demanded that the government not prolong the agreement beyond 1970. This time, however, there was no significant outspoken support from either the labor unions—except for the most radical groups such as the Dohroh (unions of the national railroads' locomotive drivers) and the combative Japanese teachers' unions, together called Nikkyoso—or the majority of opinion leaders and intellectuals. There were some extreme ideologists and radical students on university campuses. The most violent of these students became the Japanese Red Army. They were ideologically much more radical than the leaders of Zengakuren in 1960, but their activities were completely confined to the universities, with little outside support. They may be regarded as having simply played at a pseudo-war. The movement this time was somewhat encouraged, however, by the sentiment in Japan as well as in the United States against the Vietnam War and also by the sympathy of radical students, intellectuals, and journalists with the Cultural Revolution movement in China. In fact, some of the student leaders were trained in China and sent back to Japan with the intention of inciting previously nonpolitical students to revolutionary action in Japan.

Despite these circumstances, however, the political turbulence hardly affected the continuous growth of the Japanese economy. When the Vietnam War ended, with the victory of North Vietnam, there was again some excitement on the part of radical groups. But it remained a short episode in the success story of 10 percent growth. Optimism prevailed among most Japanese economists and politicians, and very few expected much change in this course of development for another decade or so. Sudden change, however, followed in the next period.

The shock period.   The *first shock* was the so-called Nixon shock, which consisted of three things. The first was the embargo of soy beans, which awakened the Japanese to the importance of security for the food supply. The second was the sudden revaluation of the yen from a fixed rate of 360 yen per dollar to a rate of 270 yen to the dollar. How unsophisticated the Japanese bankers and fiscal policy makers were then was demonstrated by the fact that the Tokyo foreign exchange market remained open for a day after the major foreign exchange markets had closed all over the world. The third shock occurred when the United States secretly negotiated with Communist China over the heads of the Japanese government.

This "Nixon shock" made the Japanese government and political leaders reevaluate the degree of trust existing between the United States and Japan. In the minds of most Japanese leaders, it may be pointed out here, the greatest mistake of prewar Japan was to have fought against China on the Asian mainland and the most crucial key to peace in East Asia was, is, and will be friendly relations between Japan and China. At the same time the leaders had not forgotten the great potential of the

Chinese resources and markets. They interpreted the U.S. action as a "go" signal to China. Prime Minister Tanaka dashed to China and signed the Japan-China Joint Declaration to resume diplomatic relations, only seven months after President Nixon's visit. Thus, the Japanese government, without appropriate caution about keeping up good relations with the Republic of China (on Taiwan) and without careful consideration of the solid base needed for lasting peace between China and Japan, concluded a peace treaty with China in 1978, one year earlier than the United States.

The *second shock* was the first oil shock, in 1972 and 1973. Perhaps this was the most serious shock to the Japanese nation since World War II. Many elderly Japanese were reminded of the wartime shortage of everything. In a town near Osaka so many housewives queued up to buy toilet paper that they exhausted the supply in one day. Prime Minister Miki hurried to visit countries in the Middle East. The government tightened the belt of public expenditure and put a sudden brake on the rapidly growing Japanese economy. The growth rate of GNP became zero in 1973 and thereafter rose only to about half its previous level. Overall, then, the GNP growth rate went from 11 percent in the 1960s to 6 percent in the early 1970s; and the rate of inflation became as high as 30 percent (at the annual rate) for several months. This made the previously complacent Japanese realize again how vulnerable the Japanese economy fundamentally is, depending as it does on an imported supply of energy from the faraway Persian Gulf. The importance of an assured energy supply as the second element of the nation's security was clearly marked in the minds of the Japanese leaders and common people alike.

The *third shock* was the second oil shock in 1978 and 1979. This time, however, the Japanese response to the oil price hike was different. From the experiences after the first oil shock the Japanese government and businesses came to realize that oil was available—for a price—and that the higher the price went, the greater the supply became. Hence, the government did not simply adopt belt-tightening policies. Needless to say, however, payments for oil suddenly increased, which increased efforts to drive up exports. At the same time, the Japanese fiscal deficit became very large, and the government had to reduce public expenditures for that reason. Administration reform or smaller government was advocated by many leading economists as well as politicians and became almost the national consensus. As a result of these policy directions, the growth rate of GNP slowed down further and became as low as 3 percent, half of the rate in the early 1970s.

These three shocking events broke the last taboo of journalism in postwar Japan: open discussions on national security. For the first time since World War II, the defense of sea lanes became the subject of open debate in Japanese daily newspapers. This was inconceivable even in the early 1970s.

The appropriate choice of policies and the efforts of the government, businesses, and households to meet the challenge of high oil prices made the Japanese economy the most energy-efficient economy in the world. It is amazing that the Japanese GNP could grow when the absolute quantity of oil imports was declining. This gave the Japanese exports a very competitive edge in the world market and created an enormous surplus in the Japanese balance of payments. When many developing countries, particularly most Latin American countries, some Communist countries, and the Philippines, did not manage their debt adequately, the accumulated debt became almost unmanageable by the world financial institutions as well as by governments and the businesses in those countries.

Even the United States government failed to manage its economy properly under the Reagan administration. Therefore, when the recession hit the world in 1982 and 1983, with declining oil prices, the oil-exporting countries, including the Middle East oil exporters as well as developing countries in Asia, began to suffer from a serious shortage of foreign exchange. Japan and West Germany were the only two countries in the world that could supply capital to the countries that needed it.

The internationalization period.   Now Japan is expected to play an international role like the one that was single-handedly played by the United States in the past. Japan must share such functions with the United States and the western European countries. The most popular word in Japan now to describe the role of Japan in this sense is *kokusaika,* literally translated as "internationalization." This internationalization period will be discussed further, but before that a few more remarks are in order.

Factors For Japanese and Asian Rapid Economic Growth

Ten factors for Japanese economic growth. The main reasons for rapid Japanese economic growth may be attributed to the following ten factors:

1. the high rate of capital accumulation

2. the high rate of saving

3. an industrious and well-educated labor force

4. a high rate of growth in agricultural production

5. quick understanding and improvement of foreign high technology

6. excellent management and labor relations

7. sound fiscal and monetary policies

8. excellent guidance by government industrial policy

9. the banking sector's effective counseling of private enterprise

10. political stability

Most of these factors require no explanation. The interested reader may be referred to my previously published paper, "The Challenge of the Rising Sun" in *Quadrant* 14, no. 6 (1970). What is relevant and important here is that the factors responsible for the economic development of other Asian economies are very similar to those listed here.

Ten factors for Asian economic development. In another context I had occasion to discuss the factors for Asian economic development and mentioned the following ten factors:[1]

1. the high rate of capital accumulation

2. the high rate of saving

3. the successful transfer of technology appropriate for agricultural and industrial development

4. the good quality of the labor force and a declining rate of fertility

5. export-oriented development strategies in the open economies

6. the locomotive roles of the United States and Japan

7. relatively sound fiscal and monetary policies

8. tolerable distribution of income

9. steady build-up of the bureaucracy and private enterprise as required in every stage of economic development

10. infrequent occurrence of social unrest and political instability

Among these factors, it is uniquely important that the Japanese government carefully designed its overall economic policies at three levels, as will be explained later, and that in other Asian economies the human elements of item number 4 in this list and the economic policies of the respective governments were especially noteworthy in comparison with those of the developing countries in the rest of the world. After the discussion of these aspects, some remarks will be added on the common features of Japanese development and Asian development in two respects: (a) acceleration and deceleration of growth rate and (b) income distribution in Asian economies.

Three levels of designing Japanese economic policies.   First, it may be a unique feature of Japanese policy making in development programming that policies are made distinctively at three different levels, or according to three different forms of official documents and regulations, in designing development strategies:

1. economic indicative plans

2. nationwide and regional development plans

3. industrial policies

Table 3 shows the correspondence between medium-term economic plans and regional development plans of the Japanese government throughout the postwar period.

The economic plans are usually called five-year plans or medium-term plans and announced by the Economic Planning Agency, and they are simply the indicative plans to give the predictions of the likely course of the Japanese economy in the medium run and to present the guidelines for macro fiscal and monetary policies for government agencies and private enterprises. The plans are widely circulated and read by government officials, businessmen, bankers, and university students. Often the questions for the entrance examinations of government ministries and prominent enterprises are taken from the white papers of these government economic plans. There are plenty of available discussions on Japanese macroeconomic policies, so those policies will not be taken up in this essay. The success of those policies is clearly shown by the achievement of a high growth rate with little inflation, despite the difficulties mentioned above, particularly the two oil shocks.

As for the regional development plan, it is mainly concerned with the use of national land—where to locate industries and which districts must be developed by public investment. Table 3 demonstrates how the government has dealt with regional allocation of land use in Japan. There is no doubt that the most scarce factor for Japanese economic development is land, so that the efficient use of land is the number-one problem for the long-run development of the Japanese economy. Efficiency almost by necessity leads to too much concentration of industrial activities and urbanization. The Japanese government has had, from the very beginning of postwar development as well as in the prewar days, national plans for land use. Table 3 shows how these regional development plans have been prepared and how they have guided industrial activities and enormous domestic migration during the past four decades.

These regional development policies have been guided largely by the four National Total Development Plans (Zenkoku Sogo Kaihatsu Keikaku) of 1962, 1969, 1977, and 1988, although the government had some regional development plans long before 1960. In fact many other regional plans were prepared not only by the central government but also by the prefectural governments under the guidance of the Ministry

TABLE 3   Economic Plans and Regional Development Plans

Economic plans	Development plans	Regional policy
	1945–1952	
Reconstruction Plan Interim Report (47.12)[a]	Basic Guidelines for National Land Use (45.9)[a]	1. Food production increase
Three-Year Self-Reliance Plan[a] (51.1)	Land Development Law (50)	2. Reconstruction of devastated land, infrastructure, and housing
	Hokkaido Development Plan (51.10)[b]	3. Resource development
		4. Inflation control
	1953–1960	
On Economic Self-Reliance (53.12)[a]	Preparation for National Total Development Plan (54.9)[a]	1. Construction of infrastructure for industrial development
Economic Self-Reliance Five-Year Plan (55.12)[a]	Tokyo Metro-Plan (58.7)[b]	2. Calamity prevention
New Long-Term Economic Plan (57.12)[a]	Tohoku Development Plan (58.8)[b]	3. Correction of regional income differentials
	Kyushu Development Plan (59.11)[b]	4. Appropriate relocation of industries to resolve regional differentials in concentration and sparceness.
	1960–1970	
National Income-Doubling Plan (60.12)[a]	Shikoku Development Plan (60.10)[b]	1. Prevention of too rapid urbanization
Medium-Term Economic Plan (65.1)[a]	National Total Development Plan (62.10)[a]	2. Development of new industrial centers

Economic and Social Development Plans	Regional/National Plans	Objectives
Economic and Social Development Plan (67.3)[a]	Promotion of New Industrial City Law Hokuriku Development Plan and Chugoku Development Plan (64.2)[b] Kinki Metro-Plan (65.5)[b] Chubu Metro-Plan (68.6)[b] New National Total Development Plan (69.5)[a]	3. Reduction of regional differentials in income and industrial activity 4. Preparation of Tokaido Megalopolis industrial and urban zones 5. Overcoming pollution problems
	1970–1980	
New Economic and Social Development Plan (70.5)[a] Economic and Social Fundamental Plan (73.2)[a] Economic Plan for Late 1970s (76.5)[a] New Economic and Social Total Development Seven-Year Plan (79.9)[a]	Biwa Lake Development Plan (72.12)[b] Promotion of Industrial Relocation Law (72) Okinawa Development Plan (74.6)[b] National Land-Use Plan (76.5)[a] Third National Total Development Plan (77.11)[a]	1. Reorientation of nationwide land use 2. Reduction of regional gaps in environmental conditions 3. Construction of transportation and communication network 4. Making living conditions harmonious between nature and human habitation
	1980–1990	
Prospect and Guideline for the 1980s (83.8)[a] Five-Year Plan for Economic Management (88.5)[a]	Fourth National Total Development Plan (87.6)[a]	1. Deconcentration of functions performed by Metro-Tokyo 2. Development and specialization of Tokyo and local centers 3. Multipolar use of land

a. Nationwide plans.
b. Regional plans.

of Construction or, later, the National Land Agency. These plans have been the guideposts for allocating the enormous amount of public investment in land reclamation and development of highways and special industrial throughout the country—all of which greatly benefit the chosen localities and are therefore politically very sensitive. Table 3 shows only the very first regional plans prepared for each region in Japan. Indeed, the first regional development plan was prepared to synthesize the preceding provincial development plans, particularly in less-developed areas in Japan such as Hokkaido.

In relation to these regional development plans, the postwar era is sometimes subdivided into the following periods:

1. resource development, 1945–1955

2. construction of the industrial base, 1955–1960

3. elimination of regional differentials, 1960–1972

4. reorientation of national land use, 1972–1977

5. establishing stable habitation (a stable combination of residence and job opportunities within a given area), 1977–1987

6. development with multipolar centers (growth centers other than Tokyo), 1987–

Each of these divisions roughly corresponds to the one of the periods of postwar growth of the Japanese economy that I have previously presented in this paper. The subperiod titles suggest what issues were targeted in the corresponding National Total Development Plans, which began in the third period. It must be emphasized that any preferential treatment in public investment was based on one of the special laws named in Table 3; otherwise, any regionally differential treatment would have been very limited. The government has tried very hard to mitigate the concentration of industrial activities in certain areas, particularly around established urban centers such as Tokyo, Nagoya, or Osaka. It is well known, nevertheless, that the Japanese economy was unable to avoid concentration of industrial and other activities around Tokyo. That is the reason why the Fourth National Total Development Plan explicitly mentions the idea of "multipolar dispersed use of national land." It does not seem, however, that the Fourth Plan (the latest) can be carried out unless it is substantiated by political decisions in the form of laws to promote decentralization or dispersion of industrial and political activities now located in Tokyo.

The third level of Japanese economic policies is now well known as industrial policy. It may be regarded as a supply side policy to overcome market failure—an approach that was practiced successfully in Japan long before the debate on supply side economics in the United States and the somewhat unsuccessful introduction of such policies under the Reagan administration. It had two clear purposes: first, to develop the export industries critically important in each stage of development and, second, to help the declining industries restructure themselves, as well as to help medium-sized and small enterprises improve their technologies and management so as to survive in the ever-changing industrial world. The tools and measures of industrial policy have changed over time. It must be emphasized that substantial supports to some selected industries, such as the ship-building industry in the early stage or the electronics industry in the later stage, were undertaken under the special laws permitting the government to give preferential treatment to those industries. However, relatively less important support to some industries or coordination or reconciliation of industries' interests were often undertaken as "administrative guidance" by the Ministry of International Trade and Industry. One cannot claim that in all cases the government industrial policies have been successful; but in many cases they seem to have guided the course of Japanese industrial restructuring and to have succeeded particularly well in helping declining industries to die less painfully and in making small and medium-sized enterprises adjust their production lines soon enough to survive and move up-market with progressing technologies. There are many valuable works on this subject in Japanese, so I shall not repeat their discussions here; I simply point out the importance of this level of Japanese economic policies.[2]

Japanese economic policies have been coordinated at these three levels. The macropolicies (the first level) were primarily the responsibility of the Ministry of Finance and the Bank of Japan. The regional

development policies (the second level) are the responsibility of the
Ministries of Construction, Transportation, and Communication. In order
to coordinate their respective policies better, a new agency, the National
Land Agency, was created in 1980. The industrial policies (the third level)
are undertaken by the Ministries of International Trade and Industry (for
manufacturing industries) and of Agriculture, Fishery, and Forestry (for
primary industries). No ministry is quite responsible for consumers in
Japan; a bureau in the Economic Planning Agency has responsibility
to monitor the living conditions of the nation and publishes a *White Paper
on National Living* every year. It may be added that social welfare policies
are taken care of by the Ministry of Welfare. Social welfare in Japan
by now has reached a very high level, particularly in health insurance
and unemployment insurance. This last policy has no doubt contributed
to the recent stability in labor relations and has helped to extinguish social
unrest in Japan in recent years.

Contributions of human factors to Asian development.   The
human and social aspects of Asian countries may be seen in Table 4.

As these figures and more recent data show, the education investment
in human capital is very impressive in most Asian countries. There is
no doubt that all Asian Pacific countries have emphasized education and
have thereby improved the quality of performance by workers, engineers,
salaried persons, executives, government officials, and intellectuals. The
majority of workers in these countries now have secondary education,
and there are enough middle managers and engineers to facilitate the
transfer of higher technologies. In particular, Korea is outstanding. Among
the ASEAN-4 Indonesia is significantly behind, and Malaysia is behind
others particularly in higher education. In most East and Southeast Asian
countries secondary education is so widespread that most factories have
no difficulty in employing workers with this level of education. As a
result, the transfer of technology and training for new technologies can
be done with little difficulty, and such recently developed devices as
QC (quality control) circles can be easily introduced in Asian NIEs.
By way of comparison in South Asia only Sri Lanka and Myanmar have
made such an extraordinary educational effort and thereby achieved such
a high literacy rate.

TABLE 4 Indices of Social Development in Asian Countries (percentage)

	Literacy		Newspaper subscriptions		Primary education		Secondary education		Higher education	
	1970	1985	1970	1985	1965	1985	1965	1982	1965	1985
I. Asian economies										
Japan	99	99	520	569a	100	102	82	96	13	30
NIEs										
Singapore	72	86	200	279	105	115	45	71	10	12
Hong Kong	77	88	498	560	103	105	29	69	5	13
Taiwan	85	92	—	—	98	100	59	80	8	18
Korea	88	96a	136	192a	101	96	35	94	6	32
ASEAN-4										
Malaysia	58	73	75	173	90	99	28	53	2	6
Thailand	79	91	20	52	78	97	14	30	2	20
Philippines	83	86	14	37	113	106	41	65	19	38
Indonesia	57	74	—	14	72	118	12	39	1	7
Giant economies										
China	43	69a	—	19	89	124	24	39	0	2
India	33	43	16	19	74	92	27	35	5	9

(continued on next page)

TABLE 4 (continued)

	Literacy		Newspaper subscriptions		Primary education		Secondary education		Higher education	
	1970	1985	1970	1985	1965	1985	1965	1982	1965	1985
South Asia										
Pakistan	21	29	–	18	40	47	12	17	2	5
Sri Lanka	78	87	49	106	93	103	35	63	2	5
Myanmar	66a	81	9	14	71	102	15	24	1	4
Nepal	13	25	2	7	20	79	5	25	1	5
Bangladesh	23	33	–	6a	49	60	13	18	1	5
Socialist economies										
Vietnam	–	84b	–	8	–	100	–	43	–	3
Kampuchea	–	–	–	–	77	–	9	–	1	–
Laos	44a	84	–	–	40	97	2	18	(.)	(.)
North Korea	–	–	–	–	–	–	–	–	–	–
II. Latin American economies										
Argentina					101	108	28	70	14	36
Brazil					108	104	16	35	2	11
Chile					124	109	34	69	6	16
Colombia					84	117	17	50	3	13

NOTES: Figures for newspaper subscription are per thousand. Blank cell = not applicable; dash = not available; (.) = too small.
a. 1980.
b. 1979.

The health of workers also has improved substantially. While calorie intake differs among the different groups of economies, the majority of workers in every country now get more than the required minimum daily amount of calories so that they can work as hard as they are willing to.

Another important feature contributing to the improvement of the quality of labor in the region is that demographic transition has been successfully progressing in almost every country and subregion. Here again, however, the gaps between the groups are significant enough to reflect the effects of policy differences on population. There seems to be a high mutual correlation in these countries between the level of per capital GNP and the fertility rate, with the exception of China, where a population policy has been particularly aggressively pursued.

Open-door and liberalization policy orientation. As for the economic policies in developing countries, three domestic policy directions and three external conditions seem to be crucial for the successful realization of economic development (see Table 5).

On the domestic economic policies:

1. Fundamentally the policy is to open the national economy to the outside world and adopt liberal policies for international trade, foreign direct investment, and international finance.

2. Government policies are basically oriented to growth, especially export-oriented growth.

3. The foreign exchange rate is maintained below the purchasing parity level for exportable price-elastic products, so that exports are promoted, imports restrained, and capital inflow encouraged.

On the international environments:

1. The trading partners' markets are open for their imports under the conditions of free competition.

TABLE 5 Characteristics of Economic Policies in Asian Countries

| | Trade | | Capital | | Finance | | Exchange Rate | |
	Export promotion	Import liberalization	Permit regulations	Joint venture regulations	Permit regulations	Loan regulations	Undervalued	Flexible
Japan	A	B	A	A	A	A	A	A
Asian NIES								
Singapore	A	A	A	A	A	A	B	B
Hong Kong	A	A	A	A	A	A	A	B
Taiwan	A	B	B	B	A	B	B	B
Korea	A	B	B	B	A	B	B	B
ASEAN-4								
Malaysia	B	B	B	B	A	B	B	B
Thailand	B	B	B	B	A	B	B	B
Philippines	B	B	C	C	C	C	C	C
Indonesia	B	B	C	C	B	C	B	B+
Giant economies								
China	B	C	C⁻	C⁻	C⁻	C⁻	C	C
India	B	C	C⁻	C⁻	C⁻	C⁻	C	C

South Asia

Sri Lanka	C	C	C–	C–	C–	C	C
Pakistan	C	C	C–	C–	C–	C	C
Myanmar	C	C	C–	C–	C–	C	C
Nepal	C	C	C–	C–	C–	C	C
Bangladesh	C	C	C–	C–	C–	C	C

NOTE: A = satisfactory; B = slightly restrictive; C = very restrictive; C– = extremely restrictive.

2. The supply, offer, or transfer of capital equipments, technology, management know-how, and capital funds is freely
   and generously made to developing countries.

3. The law and order needed for free and fair trade and transactions are not disturbed by political or military conflicts.

Since the external conditions are more or less common to all the
countries, what is more important for the purpose of development is
the domestic policies of the respective countries. My own personal
evaluation of each Asian country around 1987 on these scores is
shown in Table 5. There is no doubt that some Asian countries liberalized
the restrictions and regulations of permit for trade, direct investment,
and loans.

It would seem that the more restrictive the policies of a country have
been, the less successful the economic development performance of that
country has been. It would seem crucial to have liberal, open policies
for direct investment at an early stage of development to counter some
special-interest business groups in each country. Some Asian countries
seem to need a reconsideration of their policies on these matters.

**Acceleration and deceleration of the growth rate in Asian
development.** A noticeable feature of Asian growth is its acceleration
since the 1960s. In the 1950s even East Asian countries by no means
gave the impression to such famous economists as Rosenstein Rodan
that they would achieve the impressive growth that we have observed.
This is due not only to the high rate of capital accumulation and the
high rate of saving but also, as can be seen from Table 6, to the increase
in those rates as per capita incomes of those countries go up.

A steady increase in the rate of capital accumulation has been
characteristic of Japan's history for the past one hundred years. Nevertheless, the prewar Japanese rate of capital accumulation did not exceed
15 percent of GNP, whereas in postwar years the ratio has risen from
14.6 percent in 1953 to a high of 32 percent in 1965 and leveled off at
28–30 percent in the early 1980s. In the Asian Pacific NIEs and the
ASEAN-4 the ratio of capital formation to GNP increased from somewhat

TABLE 6   Rates of Capital Accumulation and Saving in Selected Asian-Pacific Economies, 1965–1986

	GNP per capita 1986 (U.S. dollars)	Rate of capital accumulation (percentage)				Rate of saving (percentage)			
		1965–72	1973–78	1979–83	1986	1965–72	1973–78	1979–83	1986
Industrial market economy									
Japan	12,840	31.9	35.9	32.0	28.0	30.8	33.6	36.8	32.0
NIES									
Singapore	7,410	36.7	34.9	40.4	40.0	23.6	32.8	35.6	40.0
Hong Kong									
Taiwan	4,000	26.2	30.6	32.4	—	23.1	29.3	37.0	—
S. Korea	2,370	24.1	29.0	30.0	29.0	14.9	24.9	23.7	35.0
Developing economies									
Malaysia	1,830	19.6	25.7	33.4	25.0	20.8	27.2	26.3	32.0
Thailand	810	23.8	25.4	25.3	21.0	21.3	23.6	20.5	25.0
Philippines	560	20.9	28.6	29.6	13.0	17.1	23.9	23.3	19.0
Indonesia	490	12.6	20.6	23.0	26.0	6.9	18.8	20.1	21.0
Giant economy									
China	300	—	—	33.6	39.0	—	—	33.2	36.0

(continued on next page)

TABLE 6 (continued)

	GNP per capita 1986 (U.S. dollars)	Rate of capital accumulation (percentage)				Rate of saving (percentage)			
		1965–72	1973–78	1979–83	1986	1965–72	1973–78	1979–83	1986
Latin American economies									
Venezuela	2,920	29.1	35.4	26.2	20.0	29.8	36.1	29.3	21.0
Argentina	2,350	20.4	24.6	20.5	9.0	20.3	26.2	17.9	11.0
Mexico	1,860	21.3	23.4	26.1	21.0	19.2	20.2	24.2	16.0
Brazil	1,810	25.6	28.1	22.5	21.0	24.0	24.0	17.6	24.0
Chile	1,320	15.3	15.3	17.2	15.0	13.0	11.9	7.0	18.0
Ecuador	1,160	18.6	26.4	24.2	20.0	11.3	20.4	20.5	20.0
Colombia	1,139	19.0	18.8	20.0	18.0	15.4	19.1	17.2	20.0
Peru	1,090	16.7	16.0	17.0	20.0	15.2	11.4	13.5	18.0

NOTES: Figures for Taiwan are for 1970 instead of 1965; those for Singapore are for 1982 instead of 1983. Dash = not available.
SOURCES: World Development Report, 1985, 1986, 1988; National Statistical Yearbooks.

below 20 percent in the 1960s to nearly 30 percent or even more in the early 1980s.

The rates of saving in our sample countries have also been very high. The saving ratio went up quickly from about 16 percent of GNP in the late 1960s to over 20 percent of GNP in the early 1980s. In Taiwan and Singapore it has been even higher than the Japanese gross saving rate of about 30 percent, special policies of government in these two countries having played an important role. In Singapore forced saving through a device called the Central Provident Fund is responsible for the high rate, whereas in Taiwan it is government saving that is particularly high. Apart from these two cases, however, the household saving rates are also very significant in most of our sample. This steady increase in the rates of capital accumulation and saving, with rising per capita income over the past three decades, is the most fundamental characteristic of the Asian Pacific economies; and it is the fundamental cause of acceleration of the growth rate in Asian countries.[3]

Even if the rate of capital accumulation is high, rapid growth may not result unless capital is efficiently utilized. The so-called incremental capital-output ratio (ICOR)—the amount of additional capital required to increase gross domestic product by an additional unit—is an overall index of efficiency in the use of capital.[4] Usually, as per capita income goes up the ICOR increases. Table 7 shows that this is true for all our Asian Pacific countries. But the increases have been relatively mild owing to their successful learning of modern technology. Taiwan especially has kept an impressively low ratio. The Indonesian ICOR, though low, must be considered relatively high for a country with Indonesia's low per capita income. South Korea, with a per capita income slightly lower than Taiwan's, nevertheless has an ICOR slightly higher, mainly because it has adopted deliberate policies to emphasize heavy chemical industries. Malaysia and Singapore have high ICORs corresponding to their high and rising per capita incomes. The Philippines, with an income level similar to that of Thailand, has an ICOR as high as Japan's.

Despite the variations in the rates of capital accumulation (the ratios of capital formation to GDP and to the values of ICOR), there seems to be a general trend in most Asian economies, including Japan. The ratio of capital formation to GDP tends first to increase

TABLE 7   International Comparison of Incremental Capital-Output Ratio, 1965–1983

	1965–1973			1974–1983		
	Growth rate (percentage)	Rate of accumulation (percentage)	ICOR	Growth rate (percentage)	Rate of accumulation (percentage)	ICOR
Industrial market economy						
Japan	9.8	30.0	3.1	4.3	22.7	5.2
Asian NIEs						
Singapore	13.0	36.7	2.8	8.2	37.6	4.6
Hong Kong						
Taiwan	10.1	26.2	2.6	8.5	31.5	3.7
South Korea	10.0	24.1	2.4	7.3	29.5	4.0
ASEAN-4						
Malaysia	6.7	19.6	2.9	7.3	29.1	4.0
Thailand	7.8	23.8	3.1	6.9	25.4	3.7
Philippines	5.4	20.9	3.9	5.4	29.1	5.4
Indonesia	8.1	12.6	1.6	7.0	21.8	3.1
Giant economies						
China						
India	3.9	18.3	4.7	4.0	23.2	5.8

South Asia						
Pakistan	5.4	16.3	3.0	5.6	15.9	2.8
Sri Lanka	4.2	16.1	3.8	5.2	23.1	4.4
Myanmar	—	—	—	5.5	15.8	2.8
Nepal	—	—	—	3.7	13.8	3.7
Bangladesh	—	—	—	5.2	9.4	1.8
Socialist economies						
Vietnam	—	—	—	—	—	—
Kampuchea	—	—	—	—	—	—
Laos	—	—	—	—	—	—
North Korea	—	—	—	—	—	—
Latin American economies						
Argentina	4.3	20.4	4.7	0.4	22.6	56.4
Brazil	9.8	25.8	2.6	4.8	25.3	5.3
Chile	3.4	15.3	4.5	2.9	16.3	5.6
Colombia	6.4	19.0	3.0	3.9	19.4	5.0
Mexico	7.9	21.3	2.7	5.6	24.7	4.4
Peru	3.5	16.7	4.8	1.8	17.5	9.7
Venezuela	5.1	29.1	5.7	2.5	25.8	10.3

Blank cell = not applicable; dash = not available.
SOURCES: *World Development Report*, 1985 and 1986; National Statistical Yearbooks; Asian Development Bank, *Key Indicators of Developing Member Countries of ADB* (July 1989).

and then decrease, as per capita GDP goes up. The value of ICOR seems to show a trend to increase as per capita GDP goes up, but the degree of increase seems to differ significantly from one economy to another. This implies, then, that if the demand for GDP more or less matches the increasing level of capacity of the national economy, the rate of growth in productive capacity expressed in real GDP in each national economy has a trend of acceleration at an early stage of development and deceleration in later stages. A simple formula will be the following:

$$dY/Y \text{ (Growth rate of } Y) = I/Y \text{ (Rate of capital accum.)} \div I/dY \text{ (ICOR)}$$

where the rate of capital accumulation has the reversed ∪ shape as a function of per capita GDP, fundamentally reflecting the similar shape in the savings function as depending on per capita income; and ICOR is an increasing function of per capita GDP. Since the growth rate of GDP *minus* the rate of increase in population is the growth rate of per capita GDP, we can reduce this equation to a simple nonlinear differential or difference equation for per capita GDP, ignoring the difference between GNP and GDP for the time being. If the functional shapes of I/Y and ICOR as a function of per capita GDP are not too complicated, one can derive the passage of Y over time by solving the equation. But without going through such calculation, it can be seen that the growth rate of GDP will go up if I/Y increases while ICOR remains unchanged or increases only slightly. This seems to have been the case in most Asian developing countries.

Fortunately most of the countries had saving ratios high enough to allow them to grow fast without relying as much on foreign loans as Latin American countries did. But if ICOR goes up, as was the case in the Philippines or most south Asian countries, acceleration of the growth rate cannot take place. As per capita income goes up further, I/Y begins to taper off and ICOR starts going up, so that the growth rate slows down. This has been the case in Japan and some newly industrializing economies in recent years.

From these observations one may get the impression that even in the Asian Pacific countries capital may be excessively utilized and that the ideal value should have been something like Taiwan's. But India has an extremely high ICOR despite its low income level, implying that it has inefficient use of capital. ICOR values in Latin America also are particularly high. Even if we consider the conditions of debt-ridden recession, still their ICORs are too high, because even if we assume hypothetically that the growth rate for 1974–1983 remained the same as that for 1965–1973, the ICORs for Argentine, Peru, and Venezuela are 5.3, 5.0, and 5.1 respectively. With the exception perhaps of the Philippines, it is clear that the usage of capital has been much more efficient in the Asian Pacific region than in South Asia or Latin America.

As for technological innovation in Asia during the period under investigation, the most remarkable phenomenon is the Green Revolution, which introduced high-yielding varieties of cereals, including rice, the most important crop in the Asian Pacific region. New technology offered new opportunities to increase productivity in Asian agriculture, where the use of land was already very intensive and the potential for extensive expansion of production was very limited. This seems to have made it possible to increase agricultural production without too much capital requirement, although introduction of high-yielding varieties of rice required additional investments in fertilizer and irrigation. Had the Green Revolution not made it possible not only to increase production but also to absorb the enormous surplus of labor in the rural areas in Asia, the distribution of income and social stability would have been much worse in all agrarian areas in Asia.

Economic Growth without Serious Political Disruption

Japanese economic development was achieved not without political disruption, as I argued in "Patterns of Asian Development" above; but, considering the speed of growth, the degree of political stability maintained is impressive. Alfred Marshall warned that too-rapid growth might lead to social unrest. Simon Kuznets mentioned that economic growth had to be thought of as a process of social disruption as well as improvement of social welfare. Since the growth of the Japanese economy has been so rapid, it is no surprise for Japan to have experienced the kinds of political turbulence I have discussed. What is surprising is that the nation could manage to go through the postwar hardships with no more political disruption than it had. Why serious political instability did not result from Japanese rapid growth may be explained by the following formula adopted from Karl Deutsch's and Samuel Huntington's formulae, which are somewhat more complex.[5]

Economic discontent = Material want/Consumption
Social discontent = Economic discontent/Income distribution
Social frustration = Social discontent/Social mobility
Political instability = Social frustration/Political participation

Economic discontent in the representative Japanese household did not increase very much, thanks to the facts that most Japanese households kept their material wants modest and that rapid economic growth increased per capita consumption more than most families expected. But of course there were enough dissatisfied families. Their discontent did not spread and reach a high degree of social frustration, because income distribution in Japan remain surprisingly egalitarian. Gini ratios (percentages of income obtained by the richest 10 percent) did not deteriorate very much after the war and soon improved. Nevertheless, some degree of social discontent remained significant, particularly in urban areas, primarily due to the poor living conditions there. Evidence for discontent is also found in the fact that the opposition parties usually obtain more support in urban areas than in the countryside.

In other Asian countries, except for Taiwan, income inequality is much more serious, as Table 8 shows. There seem to be good reasons to believe that these figures probably grossly underestimate the inequality of income in most countries in Asia as well as in other parts of the world. Figures for distribution of income such as those shown may be regarded as an index expressing the sharing of welfare among various social groups that is to be derived from the growth of national income. Comparison with the degree of inequality of Japan's income distribution is perhaps an improper comparison, since Japan's is extraordinarily low even by world standards. If one compares the income distribution in the Asian countries other than Japan with that in other developing countries, one finds those in our sample to be unusually equitable. Table 8 gives the percentage of income of the richest 10 percent and 20 percent of the population and the poorest 20 percent, based on household and

TABLE 8   Income Inequality of Selected Asian Economies with Latin American Comparisons

| | Year studied | Share of total income (percentage) | | | |
		Poorest 20% of population	Richest 20% of population	Richest 10% of population	Degree of inequality
I. Asian Pacific					
Industrial market economy					
Japan	1979	8.7	37.5	22.4	5.1
NIEs					
Singapore	1975	5.4	48.9	28.7	10.1
Taiwan	1979	8.6	37.5	22.0	4.4
South Korea	1976	5.7	45.3	27.5	9.6
Hong Kong	1980	5.4	47.0	31.3	11.6
Developing economies					
Malaysia	1973	3.5	56.1	39.8	22.7
Thailand	1976	5.6	49.8	34.1	12.2
	1981	5.4	51.5	(8.9)	(9.5)
	1986	4.6	55.6	—	(12.1)
Philippines	1971	5.2	54.0	38.5	14.8
	1985	5.2	52.5	37.0	14.2
Indonesia	1976	6.6	49.4	34.0	10.3

(continued on next page)

TABLE 8   (continued)

| | Year studied | Share of total income (percentage) | | | Degree of inequality |
		Poorest 20% of population	Richest 20% of population	Richest 10% of population	
Giant economy					
China					
India	1976	7.0	49.4	33.6	9.6
II. South Asia					
Sri Lanka	1981	5.8	49.8	34.7	12.0
Bangladesh	1982	6.6	45.3	29.5	8.9
III. Latin America					
Argentina	1970	4.4	51.4	34.6	15.8
Brazil	1972	2.0	66.6	50.9	50.9
Mexico	1977	2.9	57.7	40.6	28.0
Peru	1972	1.9	61.0	42.9	45.2

NOTES: Degree of inequality is calculated as the ratio of the percentage of the richest 20 percent to that of the poorest 20 percent. Blank cell = not applicable; dash = not available.

SOURCES: *World Development Report*, 1985, 1986, 1988; National Statistical Yearbooks; Thai Development Research Institute, *Quarterly Newsletter*, 1989

expenditure surveys of various countries. The study years are different from one country to another, but they do give a rough impression that the income share of the richest 10 percent in Asia is in the 30 percent range, whereas that in Latin America is between 40 percent and 50 percent. The income share of the poorest 20 percent in Asian Pacific countries, except Japan, ranges from 3.5 percent to 6.6 percent, whereas in Latin America, with the exception of Argentina, it varies from only 1.9 percent to 2.9 percent.

If we define an index of inequality as the average income of the richest 10 percent divided by the average income of the poorest 20 percent, the indices derived are those shown in the last column of Table 8. Argentina seems to be exceptional among the Latin American countries for its relative equality. The Philippines and Malaysia seem to be exceptional among the Asian Pacific countries for their relative inequality. It is also true that the inequality in the Philippines and also Indonesia may be underestimated by these data (S. Ichimura, *Indonesian Economic Development* [Tokyo: Japan International Cooperation Agency, 1987]). It is not reasonable to suppose, therefore, that income distribution poses no problems in the region. Nevertheless, even with these qualifications, one cannot escape the conclusion that in general the income distribution in the societies of our sample is much more egalitarian than that in the societies of Latin America.

As for the relationship between economic growth and income inequality, the inverted ∪-shaped relation of Simon Kuznets is well known; income distribution tends to worsen in the early stages of industrialization until a turning point is reached at some level of per capita income. By comparing the income inequality indices of Asian countries with the fertility rate, the share of employment in agriculture, the improvement of the level of education, and other economic variables, one can obtain the following correlations in the region:

1. The famous Kuznets hypothesis seems to hold for most countries, but not for Japan and Taiwan. Japan may have already passed a critical point. Taiwan may have a special circumstance because land ownership is in the hands of Taiwanese farmers, and they could obtain a significant share of industrialization benefits from the rising prices of land

and rent. This contrasts with the conditions of land ownership in the Philippines and Thailand.

2. Countries with higher fertility rates tend to have worse income distribution.

3. Among countries at similar per capita levels, those with higher shares of employment in agriculture tend to have worse income distribution.

4. Improvement of the level of education has a positive correlation with the improvement of per capita income and income distribution.

In the Asian economies that include a wide range of farmers working small and medium-size farms, of proprietors, and of enterprises, this relative inequality was mitigated when the economies developed primarily by successful agriculture and labor-intensive manufacturing industries. Taiwan and Japan are the typical cases. In other countries, where large corporations or state enterprises are conspicuously dominant, income inequality will increase pent-up social frustration. Serious social unrest has to be expected in such circumstances.

Such social discontent was mitigated by the high degree of social mobility in postwar Japanese society. Very few Japanese would doubt that graduates from good universities had equal opportunities in the best private businesses and in the government bureaucracy. The percentage of the population going on to higher education in Japan is almost as high as that in the United States and higher than that of any representative European country in terms of enrollment numbers. Needless to say, some social frustration, especially among urban workers and dissatisfied farmers, has been reduced by various forms of political participation, such as strikes, demonstrations, or the occasional success of the opposition parties in local elections. But the free and fair voting in Japan seems to have done the most to give frustrated citizens ways to participate in politics. This participation has mitigated political discontent and has kept Japanese domestic politics reasonably stable so far.

Japanese Economic Cooperation for Asian Development

As I argued in the first section of this paper, "Patterns of Asian Development," Japan is now in the period of internationalization. This period of internationalization is the one in which the Japanese economy must take initiatives to play a leading role in world economic affairs, particularly in the Asian Pacific area. The roles that Japan has played in promoting the economic development of Asian countries may be summarized as follows:

The role in international trade.

1. Japan has supplied the capital equipment needed for industrialization of Asian economies and has often offered maintenance services.

2. In the initial stages of industrialization Japan supplied the intermediate products for the import-substitution industries in Asian developing countries.

3. Japan imported primary commodities and a limited amount of manufactured goods. The share of manufactured goods in the country's total imports has increased very significantly in recent years.

4. Japan is beginning to liberalize completely the import of consumption goods and to share prosperity with the other Asian economies. If the current rate of increase in Japanese imports of manufactured goods continues, the absolute amount will approach the level of United States imports of the same commodities by the mid-1990s.

The role in international direct investment.

1. As Professor Kiyoshi Kojima has pointed out, Japanese direct investment has been handled considerably in the sense of keeping in conformity with the direction of industrial investment required by each national economy for its

development. Owing to the yen revaluation, significant relocation of Japanese industries to neighboring countries has been taking place in recent years.

2. Japanese businesses have been more positive than American or European companies in establishing joint ventures with East and Southeast Asian enterprises.

3. Japanese companies and joint ventures tend to be more cooperative with governments' policies for industrialization, such as the *bumi putra* ("natives first") policies of Malaysia and Indonesia.

The role in international finance.

1. The Japanese government has been extensively offering official loans both bilaterally, through Overseas Economic Cooperation Funds and the Export-Import Bank, and multilaterally, through the Asian Development Bank and the World Bank.

2. Japanese private banks have also been very positive in extending loans to Asian private enterprises and foreign banks independently and, as syndicate members, in cooperation with foreign private banks.

3. The Japanese government has made very positive contributions to efforts by the multilateral institutions, such as the World Bank and the IMF, to extend soft loans to debt-ridden LDCs all over the world.

The role in technology transfer.

1. Along with the industrial restructuring and relocation of Japanese plants in neighboring countries and the establishment of joint ventures abroad, the transfer of technology, management know-how, and key engineering personnel has been taking place between Japan and other Asian countries.

2. Within the joint ventures as well as in subsidiaries of Japanese enterprises, training on the job has been offered very effectively and has contributed to the increase of labor productivity and management efficiency.

3. Japanese enterprises have successfully and effectively established subcontracting relations with companies in neighboring Asian countries and have gradually built up complementary business relations with other Asian enterprises. This may turn out to be very effective in increasing intraregional trading relations in the near future.

The role in resource and information transfer.

1. In promoting mutual business relations the transfer of human resources, including managers, engineers, and other experts, is very important, in addition to the export of material resources.

2. Japan often plays the role of intermediary between the modern world and other Asian countries by transferring or exporting information on economic matters, technology, and business, as well as academic or cultural knowledge through education, books, and various publications. This transfer is very important in minimizing the time and effort needed to learn better ways of carrying out economic and social development. The annual number of publications in Japanese is almost equivalent to the number of publications in the United States. Korean and Taiwan business circles may have benefited more in these respects than have other Asian countries' businesses.

3. The temporary migration of unskilled or semiskilled labor to Japan that is taking place nowadays is almost inevitable. This issue will become more prominent in the near future, since the income differentials are widening so much between Japan and some other Asian countries. The income transfer due to this migration will be too significant to be ignored.

The role in economic cooperation.

1. The Japanese government has been rapidly expanding its
   official development assistance (ODA) particularly after the
   yen revaluation. The absolute amount of this aid exceeded
   the U.S. aid (in U.S. dollars) in 1989, but its proportion in
   GNP is still not very high.

2. The proportion of technical cooperation in ODA is not very
   large. The main parts consist of the grant elements in loans.
   Critics say that Japan gives money but not enough sweat,
   and no blood at all. At the same time, it is still true that some
   in Asia as well as in the United States fear the revival of a
   militarily strong Japan, even at this stage of history.

In the circumstances I have described, the role Japan may be expected
to play in the future may be summarized in the eight points that follow.
For a fuller description, see the appendix to this essay.

1. Japan is a pacemaker and caretaker in the Asian Pacific
   region; therefore, Japanese economic policies must be
   determined not only for the development of the Japanese
   economy itself but also according to the requirements of the
   world economy and particularly of the economies of closely
   related neighboring countries.

2. Japan must play a leading role in restructuring the industrial
   composition of economies at different stages of development,
   while keeping the income gaps among the nations within a
   tolerable range. For this purpose it is critically important to
   open up the Japanese domestic markets for manufactured
   goods and for many activities in the service industries.

3. Japan must play the role of adviser—even on other countries'
   domestic economic policies—on the basis of its own experience and study of modernization and industrialization.

4. Japan must do its best to maintain the institutions for free
   trade and the flow of goods, services, finance, capital,

information, and labor, as much as it is politically feasible to do so.

5. Japan must be a mediator, whenever needed, between Asian developing countries and other powers in the world—for example, in helping to find satisfactory places for Asian NICs among the industrialized countries.

6. Japan must play an important role beyond the Asian Pacific region in extending economic cooperation to supplement the roles of the United States and the European Community in the world.

7. Japan must be prepared to participate more actively in the international institutions by contributing more capital, personnel, and knowledge, always in cooperation with the United States and the EC.

8. For all these purposes Japan must solidly establish itself, step by step, as a reliable partner in the Western alliance.

Japanese Investment and Japanese-Style Management

In almost all items listed for Japanese international cooperation in the preceding section, private enterprises play crucial roles. The role of private enterprises is particularly critical in foreign direct investment. In most Asian countries Japan has become number one in foreign direct investment as well as public and private loans, for which the World Bank is usually number two. Since direct foreign investment brings in new technology and introduces a management style, the role played by private businesses is much more than just capital sharing. At the same time it implies foreign ownership of the national wealth and therefore touches on the sentiment of nationalism, especially in a new nation that was a foreign colony only a few decades back. Anti-Japanese riots during Prime Minister Kakuei Tanaka's visit to Thailand and Indonesia in 1974 left a deep impression in this respect on many Japanese. Prior to these outbursts, not many Japanese corporations realized that the high demand for and prevalence of their products in the region was creating the fear that local economies were being dominated by Japan. Local businesses were afraid that they would be squeezed out by Japanese firms.

This problem goes far beyond simple economic troubles and may reflect the underlying culture conflicts between Japan and other Asian nations. Many Japanese businessmen hardly recognized this possibility before. After experiencing the anti-Japanese riots, however, they have come to realize that even if the more obvious economic problems were solved, the underlying frictions might manifest themselves in other forms. Nevertheless, businessmen must carry on their activities abroad using the Japanese style of management, because it is the only management style they know and have confidence in. With an ever-larger number of Japanese firms setting up operations in Southeast Asia, it has become critically important to learn if these firms' management style is compatible with local cultures. A five-year study of ours, undertaken in two steps, shows that, with adaptations, the Japanese management system is taking root in Asia.

Japanese managers' view of Japanese management in Asia.   The first study was undertaken as part of a comprehensive research project supported by the Ministry of Education, "Culture Conflict between Japan and Other Asian Nations." This project covered not only economic conflicts, as in our study, but also many other types of conflicts since the Meiji era. For example, it dealt with the anti-Japanese sentiments and movement among Chinese students in Japan. Our own study used questionnaire survey methods to find out the conflicts in business activities in Southeast Asia from the experiences of Japanese top managers who stayed in Southeast Asia more than two years and were back home. The main findings were reported as a book, *Nihonteki Kigyo in Ajia* (Japanese firms in Asia) (Tokyo: Toyokeizai-Shimposha, 1980), whose English summary was published as "Japanese Firms in Asia," *Japanese Economic Studies,* Fall 1981. Two of the main findings may be recounted here to show the types of answers we found in this study.

To what extent has Japanese-style management been revised?   How well is the Japanese management of joint-venture firms operating in alien cultural and social circumstances? Can the characteristics of Japanese-style management be adapted to the requirements of such circumstances and conditions? If so, to what extent? At this stage we focused on four major characteristics of Japanese management:

1. lifetime employment

2. the seniority-based wage system

3. firm-based labor unions

4. the *ringi* system (decision making based on preliminary consultation with the staff)

We asked if firms tried to modify these four elements of Japanese-style management. Their answers are shown in Table 9. It is clear from Table 9 that most firms opted for revised management. The actual implementation of Japanese-style management is such that, more often than not, it is applied with modifications to meet local requirements. The four main features are substantially modified, but quite a few operate with only minor modifications: 38 percent for lifetime employment, 40 percent for the seniority wage system, and 31 percent for the ringi system. The exception is the firm-based labor union, which is adopted in only 18 percent of the firms surveyed. In this respect there is a substantial difference between Japan and Southeast Asia. To sum up, there are two groups of firms among Japanese joint ventures, one group adheres to Japanese-style management with only minor modifications,

TABLE 9   Localization of Japanese-Style Management (percentage)

	Lifetime employment	Wage system	Labor union	Ringi system
No revision	9.8	3.4	7.2	8.0
Minor revision	28.0	36.7	9.8	23.1
Major revision	12.5	42.4	14.0	12.1
Not adopted	45.1	12.1	62.1	50.0
No answer	4.5	5.3	6.8	6.3

NOTE: Deviations from 100 percent totals due to rounding.

while the other group gives it up or modifies it substantially in order to adapt more fully to local requirements.

What promotion formula is used? In modifying the Japanese management system there are significant differences from one country to another. As an example, Table 10 shows how the promotion formula in Japanese firms is modified in each Southeast Asian country. Table 10 shows that the Japanese promotion system is best practiced in Indonesia, followed by Thailand and Malaysia. Management in the Philippines is most different from the Japanese-style management, as Philippine business communities are always different from those in the other Southeast Asian countries in economic behaviors. Further study is required to determine whether this is due to the predominant influence of American businesses, the retained Spanish heritage, or the lesser number of Japanese joint ventures in the Philippines.

There were some criticisms on this initial study:

1. It exclusively relied on the views of Japanese businessmen, leaving out the opinions of local businessmen or employees.

2. The study should have covered Korea, Taiwan, and Hong Kong, which have entirely different cultural and social structures.

3. Japanese firms in Asia should be compared with American and European firms in their business behaviors in order to make a truly international comparison.

Japanese-style management taking hold in Asia. In order to meet these criticisms a second study was undertaken with the support of the Ministry of Education and the Kansai Economic Research Center, which was established by Osaka business groups. This study examined the practice of Japanese-style management in all East Asian countries, including Korea, Taiwan, and Hong Kong, as well as ASEAN countries, and surveyed not only Japanese top managers working in Southeast Asian cities but also local middle managers employed by Japanese joint ventures. We may trust that the study of the management of American and European firms will be undertaken by American and European scholars or by local

TABLE 10 Variations in Localization of Promotion Formulus (percentage)

	ASEAN	Indonesia	Malaysia	Singapore	Thailand	Philippines
Japanese system with no change	9.5	11.1	9.3	6.3	11.7	7.1
Japanese system with minor modifications	35.5	47.6	34.9	22.9	45.0	10.7
Japanese system with major modifications	16.5	11.1	16.3	25.0	16.7	14.3
Local system with no change	29.3	17.5	32.6	37.5	20.0	57.1
Entirely different systems	5.0	9.5	2.3	6.3	1.7	3.6
Flexible	4.1	3.2	4.1	2.1	5.0	7.1

NOTE: Deviations from 100 percent totals due to rounding.

research workers in cooperation with them. This second research work of ours was based on fieldwork to conduct the questionnaire surveys and interviews in each country, always in cooperation with some native scholars. The main findings are reported in a book, *Ajia-ni Nezuku Nihon-teki Keiei* (Japanese management taking hold in Asia) (Tokyo: Toyokeizai-Shimposha, 1988), whose main parts were published serially in English as *South East Asian Study* (Kyoto: Kyoto University Center for Southeast Asian Studies, 1985–1988). The bound version of these reports is available as Shinichi Ichimura, ed., *Japanese Management in Southeast Asia* (Kyoto: Kyoto University Center for Southeast Asian Studies, 1988). The interested reader is referred to these reports. Here only a few interesting parts are reproduced.

This time research was more carefully designed on the basis of the earlier study. First, Japanese-style management was characterized by its twelve elements, and their practice in Japan itself was surveyed in order to compare the degree of implementation of Japanese-style management in Japan and that in other Asian economies. Those twelve elements are:

1. stable employment

2. a seniority-based wage system

3. seniority-based promotion

4. job rotation resulting in multiskilled workers

5. emphasis on management philosophy

6. flexible management

7. collective decision making

8. collective responsibility

9. respect for human relations

10. the ringi system

11. minimal differentiation between management and workers

12. small group activities

The questionnaire surveys were conducted both in Japan and all other East Asian countries, and the actual implementation of these elements were compared among all the countries. First, the present-day practice of Japanese-style management in Japan must be observed, as is shown in Table 11.

A survey of Japanese firms in Japan revealed that though the degree of application of these principles varied from one element to another in all the companies studied, the average rate of application was only 54 percent in Japan itself. If we list the items that more than 50 percent of firms practice in the order of higher implementation, they are as follows:

1. stable employment, 86.0 percent

2. the ringi system, 82.8 percent

3. stressing management philosophy and objectives, 69.7 percent

4. small group activities, 63.9 percent

5. respect for human relations, 57.4 percent

6. job rotation, 51.6 percent

Table 11 makes it clear that the principles of group responsibility, seniority-based promotion, and minimal differentiation between management and workers are far from universally applied even among Japanese companies now.

Here we present in summarized form a comparison of the practice of Japanese-style management in other Asian economies with the findings in Japan. In order to summarize, the twelve elements are lumped together into the following four groups:

1. lifetime employment: stable employment and job rotation

2. seniority system: seniority-based wage and promotion systems

3. humanism: minimal differentiation, management philosophy, and respect for human relations

4. groupism: flexible management, group decision making, group responsibility, and small group activities

TABLE 11 The Percentage of Firms Practicing Japanese-Style Management in Japan

	All industry	Manufacturing industry			Other industry		
		Fewer than 300 employees	More than 300 employees	Total	Fewer than 300 employees	More than 300 employees	Total
1. Stable employment	86.0	80.0	90.5	84.6	83.3	90.3	88.4
2. Seniority wages	47.5	46.7	44.4	44.9	58.3	50.0	52.3
3. Seniority promotion	32.8	40.0	30.2	32.1	41.7	31.2	34.1
4. Job rotation	51.6	20.0	61.9	53.8	41.7	50.0	47.7
5. Management philosophy	69.7	60.0	69.8	67.9	75.0	71.9	72.7
6. Flexible management	48.4	60.0	49.2	51.3	25.0	50.0	43.2
7. Group decision making	42.5	40.0	49.2	47.4	33.0	34.4	34.1
8. Group responsibility	10.7	6.7	12.7	11.5	0	0	0
9. Human relations	57.4	40.0	58.3	62.8	33.3	53.1	47.7
10. Ringi system	82.8	60.0	84.1	79.5	83.3	90.6	88.6
11. Minimal differentiation	36.9	33.3	39.7	38.5	33.3	34.4	34.1
12. Small group activity	63.9	33.3	76.2	67.9	33.3	65.6	56.8
13. Others	6.6	0	6.3	5.1	8.3	9.4	9.1

Comparison of the characteristics of Japanese joint ventures operating in eight Asian countries can be shown in diagrams (see Figure 2). It is true that except for the seniority system the practice in Japan is predominant, but the difference between Japan and some other Asian economies is not as much as generally thought. In particular the management practice in Japanese affiliates in Korea, Taiwan, and Singapore were found to be very similar to those implemented in Japan. Specifically, groupism and humanism were the same in both Korean and Japanese companies, although lifetime employment and the seniority system were less common in Korea. In Taiwan humanism and the seniority system were applied in a similar manner as in Japan. Lifetime employment was practiced in the same percentage of Singaporean companies as in Japan, and humanism and groupism factors were found to only a slightly lesser degree.

A policy of localization was adopted in all countries but seems to have been given stronger emphasis in Thailand, Malaysia, Indonesia, and Korea. In actual practice, Japanese management was least emphasized in the Philippines and most comprehensively applied in Korea. Among the twelve elements of Japanese-style management, employment stabilization and management philosophy were the top two important elements in all of the countries except for Hong Kong; but there were striking differences among countries with regard to the third most important aspect of Japanese management. In most of them humanism is the third important element. This emphasis on human relations may be a central element in Japanese management and crucially important for the success of joint ventures abroad. The order of the economies where more firms emphasize human relations is: Singapore, Taiwan, Korea, Indonesia, Hong Kong, Malaysia, Thailand, and the Philippines. This sequence may reflect the degree of difficulty that the Japanese affiliates have encountered in human relations.

Labor disputes or conflicts most critically reveal the troubles of management, so the findings in our survey in this regard may be presented here, although many managers did not wish to answer on this matter. Table 12 shows the findings on the basis of the replies obtained in our survey.

Clearly Japanese joint ventures in Asia are experiencing much more labor conflict than the Japanese firms in Japan now. This will remind

Figure 2   The Actual Practice of Japanese-Style Management in Japan and Eight Asian Economies

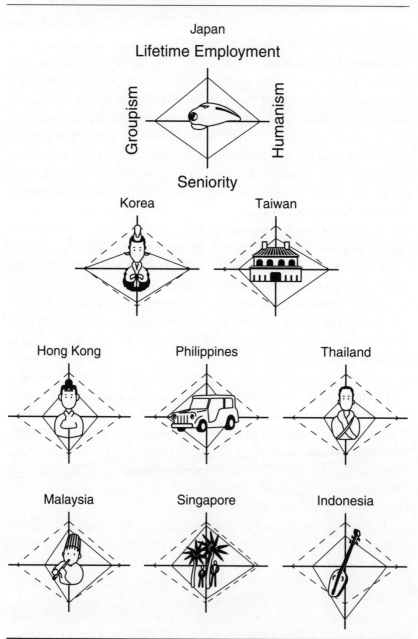

TABLE 12 The Causes of Labor Conflicts in Japanese Joint Ventures in Asia

	Japan	Korea	Taiwan	Hong Kong	Singapore	Philippines	Thailand	Malaysia	Indonesia
Sample size (number of ventures)	13	28	21	2	12	8	25	17	36
Labor conflicts experienced (%)	16.7	64.4	36.5	25.0	38.7	42.1	65.0	56.7	60.4
Wages and salaries (%)	77.0	69.0	64.0	80.0	33.0	88.0	76.0	47.0	64.0
Welfare (%)	8.0	31.0	23.0	0	8.0	25.0	44.0	6.0	11.0
Promotion (%)	0	17.0	14.0	0	17.0	0	16.0	6.0	3.0
Working hours (%)	8.0	3.0	14.0	40.0	25.0	13.0	20.0	12.0	0
Holidays (%)	0	7.0	5.0	40.0	8.0	0	12.0	18.0	3.0
Human relations (%)	0	17.0	41.0	40.0	50.0	25.0	20.0	35.0	11.0
Employment (%)	23.0	21.0	14.0	0	33.0	50.0	5.0	24.0	28.0

us of the condition of labor relations in Japan when social unrest was still prevalent in Japan some decades ago. But this may simply reflect a more complex social structure in other Asian countries and a different behavior pattern of local workers demonstrated by a high rate of job hopping. As a cause for labor disputes, the most important issue is wages and salaries; second in importance are employment issues, such as retirement or lay-offs; and the third issue is human relations. Human relations seem to be very important; the issue is number one in Singapore and number two in Malaysia, Thailand, Taiwan, and Hong Kong. In many Japanese joint ventures in other Asian countries labor unions are not organized. According to the findings of our survey, the companies without labor unions, except for those in Taiwan, seem to have experienced fewer labor conflicts.

It may be interesting to ask if the practice of Japanese-style management reduces labor conflicts. A careful observation in the case of Japanese affiliates in Taiwan seems to support the view that Japanese-style management reduces the frequency of labor disputes. Table 13 largely supports this view for Taiwan, but the evidence is not so conclusive that it precludes more careful study in the future.

This success of Japanese-style management in dealing with labor relations in other Asian countries may lead to popular support for such management practice and also for the Japanese type of firm-based labor unions in Asia.

Of course it remains to be seen if the practice of Japanese-style management can spread more widely and deeply or if local characteristics may tend to become predominant as time goes by. I believe, however, that eventually Japanese-style management will replace the American and European style of management in many Asian countries, as Japanese direct investment increases. Moreover, the Japanese market will become more and more important to Asian businesses, so that Asian business communities will come to realize they have a vested interest in learning Japanese ways of doing business. They will try to adapt to the practice of Japanese businesses, and sooner or later the local style of business practice and the Japanese style will converge. It should be remembered also that Japanese-style management itself is changing to adapt to the changing conditions of world business. As we discussed earlier, the stereotype of Japanese management is no longer the actual practice of

TABLE 13   Correlations between Japanese-Style Management and Labor
            Conflicts in Taiwan (percentage)

	Labor conflicts	
	Experienced	Avoided
Stable employment		
Yes	40.5	59.5
No	18.2	81.8
Seniority wage		
Yes	43.5	56.5
No	30.0	70.0
Seniority promotion		
Yes	31.8	68.2
No	38.7	61.3
Job rotation		
Yes	35.6	54.4
No	37.5	62.5
Flexible management		
Yes	31.6	68.4
No	38.6	61.5
Group decision making		
Yes	44.4	55.6
No	31.4	68.6
Group responsibility		
Yes	33.3	66.7
No	36.8	63.2
Human relations		
Yes	34.1	65.9
No	41.7	58.3
Ringi system		
Yes	44.4	55.6
No	25.9	73.1
Minimal differentiation		
Yes	25.0	75.0
No	40.5	59.5

Japanese-style management. Among the changes in Japan nowadays is
that the seniority-based wage and salary system is being quickly replaced
by a wage and salary system based on efficiency and ability. How
Japanese affiliates in Asia should adapt to such changing practices of

Japanese management, necessitated by conditions in Japan, is an important problem to be faced in the future. Successful businesses will always need to learn how to improve their management practice to meet the requirements of ever-changing business relations between Japanese and other Asian private enterprises.

Appendix: The Japanese Government's Official Guiding Principles for Policies for International Cooperation

The Maekawa Report is the set of official documents that Prime Minister Nakasone presented to the United States and other foreign governments as an official promise, so that their main points can be taken as the official position of the Japanese government in the future. Discussion of the main points follows.

Expanding domestic demand. In particular demand will be expanded in the following areas of activity:

1. promotion of housing investment and urban redevelopment

2. private consumption

3. infrastructure investment, especially by local governments

Transforming the industrial structure to make it internationally harmonious. The restructuring of Japanese industrial composition should be realized basically through market forces, but some additional policy direction and government guidance such as the following may be effective:

1. further promotion of current efforts to transform small and medium-sized enterprises into more technologically advanced ones (by the means available within the present legal framework), encourage research and development, and diffuse information technology

2. encouragement of overseas direct investment and bilateral agreements concerning protection of investment, such as the ones concluded recently with the Chinese government

3. promotion of agricultural policies befitting the age of internationalization

Further improving access to Japanese markets and encouraging the import of manufactured goods.   Particular aspects of changing trade policy are the following:

1. Market access must be improved much more, and more quickly, by reducing tariffs and import restrictions; adjusting standards, certification procedures, and government procurement practices; and changing many other outdated regulations.

2. The notoriously low share of Japanese imports of manufactured final products must be corrected and increased. (These have shown a remarkable increase in recent years.)

3. The number of Japanese businessmen working abroad and the number of Japanese joint ventures established with native corporations have increased very much, so that they have become integrated parts of business communities in the recipient countries. The prudent behavior of Japanese businessmen and the organizational behaviors of their companies are critical to their being received as good friends of the business communities in other countries.

Stabilizing exchange rates by international coordination and liberalizing financial and capital markets.   The following steps should be taken:

1. In maintaining the proper balance between domestic demand and supply and external demand and supply it is essential to keep the exchange rates among major currencies consistent with economic fundamentals. For this purpose the Japanese government must coordinate its policies very closely with

those of the member governments of the G-5 or G-7. This requires maintaining the proper intergovernmental conditions and exercising the appropriate interventions in the international money and capital markets. In recent years the Japanese government has been a very positive force in G-7 meetings.

2. In view of the increasing interdependence of national economies and the unprecedented amount of capital now flowing in global transactions in the international capital markets, liberalization is a necessity if the Japanese economy is to maintain strength commensurate with the important role it has to play. It is highly desirable to take measures to permit transactions by nonresidents to expand much more in the Tokyo and Osaka markets. In particular, the instruments for investment must be diversified, and the regulation of capital transactions must be made compatible with international practices in the U.S. and European markets.

Increasing Japan's contributions to international cooperation and establishing the nation's proper international status. Specific contributions are these:

1. Japanese imports of manufactured goods, particularly from developing countries, must be increased significantly, however painful it may be to Japanese industrial communities. All efforts discussed under "Further improving access to Japanese markets and encouraging the import of manufactured goods" will be essential.

2. Japan must play a leading role in resolving the debt problems of many developing countries all over the world. This must be undertaken in cooperation with the financial communities of all the other industrialized countries. Japanese experience is still very limited in these complex matters, but Japan's enormous supply of surplus capital must be handled very carefully and effectively to keep the debt problem from exploding into a great depression.

3. Japanese ODA must be expanded more and soon to exceed the average of this assistance from OECD member countries, because Japan's military burden is far less than that of the others. Japanese ODA was particularly weak in technical assistance, a condition that must be remedied as soon as possible. Promotion of international exchange in science, technology, and culture between Japan and the rest of the world should be emphasized. Japanese universities and research institutes in both the private and public sectors should be open to foreign specialists' research and training. Contributing Japan's historic heritage and contemporary culture to the world community is as important as economic cooperation for establishing Japan's proper place in the world of the future.

4. Active promotion of a new round of GATT talks is recommended. The government should positively support the establishment of international rules for trade in services and for intellectual property rights and should more actively and swiftly negotiate on tariffs and quotas on agricultural and industrial products.

Undertaking more appropriate management of fiscal and monetary policy. This should be done in the following ways:

1. In order to realize all the recommendations mentioned so far, the Japanese government must maintain the basic policy stance of achieving fiscal reform and maintaining efficient and responsible government, while mobilizing the resources and vigor of the private sector through liberalization and deregulation.

2. Tax reform will be critically important on the domestic side of Japanese economic policies. With the increasing burden that is expected from the aging population and from the international responsibilities discussed here, the Japanese government must expand the tax base and try to adjust the taxation system. Whether the government succeeds in

achieving this will have significant implications for the future
course of Japanese international cooperation as well as for
the nation's choice of domestic policies.

Conducting follow-up. It is important to point out that the
Maekawa group requested the government not only to implement these
recommended policies as soon as possible but also to follow up by
reporting how many of these recommendations have been realized.

I strongly support these recommendations and sincerely hope that
the follow-up reports will be published internationally, because these
are the government's official promises to the international community.

Economic Development, Education, and Technological Progress

Human Factors for Economic Growth

The per capita GNP of Japan in 1948 was not much above $300 in current U.S. dollars, whereas that in 1988 was about $22,000. This constitutes an average annual growth rate of 11.3 percent over forty years. The growth rate of the population and labor force has been around 1 percent through the postwar years. The growth rate of capital in real terms has been around 5 percent, so the capital per worker increased at an annual rate of about 4 percent. The difference between 11.3 percent and 4 percent must be explained by the improvement in the quality of labor, by technological progress, and by the improvement of the terms of trade and the exchange rate of the yen. The exchange rate for the yen remained at the rate of 360 Yen to 1 U.S. dollar until 1971, when it began to increase and reached 145 yen per dollar in 1990. Therefore, the gap in growth rate attributable not to the increase in factor inputs but to the quality improvement of human and technological factors in the past seventeen years is due to the revaluation of the yen, which is about 5.5 percent per year. If we discuss the average rate of increase over the forty years, then the growth rate due to the Yen revaluation is 2.3 percent. Thus, 5.0 percent—that is, 7.3 percent *minus* 2.3 percent—growth of per capita GNP must be explained by the improvement of labor quality and by technological progress.

The paper that is summarized here was presented at an international conference held at the Korea Institute for Economics and Technology (KIET), Seoul, Korea, on February 19 and 20, 1990. The Republic of Korea is facing the problem of overcoming a shortage of the skilled workers, engineers, researchers, and managers needed for further economic development. The main purpose of the conference was to make use of the Japanese postwar experiences in these matters. This essay supplies some basic information readily available in Japan.

Four Levels of Designing Japanese Economic Policies

One unique and remarkable characteristic of postwar Japanese economic policies is that they have tried to affect not only the demand side of GNP, as typical Keynesian policies do, but also the supply side as well. Specifically, decisions and programming are made at four levels:

1. economic indicative plans

2. nationwide and regional development plans

3. industrial policies

4. manpower and education plans

Here we are concerned with the last of these plans. The best documentation on manpower and education policies are the *White Paper on Labor* and the *White Paper on Education*. The basic information on education is collected by the Fundamental Survey of Education. This survey not only covers the various matters in school education as such but also aspects of the demand side of education, such as the industrial composition of graduates from high schools, colleges, and various departments of universities. Long before supply side economics was brought up as if it were something new, Japanese economists and policymakers were in full recognition of the need for and importance of the policies affecting the supply side of national product, education, and technology.

Postwar Japanese economic development can be characterized by the periodization shown in Table 14.

Japanese government and private efforts varied according to the stage of development of the national economy. But the emphasis on education and training on and off the job was noncontroversial as far back as the very beginning of the Meiji modernization.

Education and Investment in Human Capital

The improvement of labor quality has two aspects: first, education and, second, morale of the representative or average citizen. Improvement

TABLE 14   Periods of Japanese Postwar Development

	Period	Characteristics
1945–1952:	Occupation period	3 Ds (demilitarization, democratization, demonopolization), labor unions
1952–1960:	Reconstruction period	Economic and political struggles
1960–1970:	Rapid growth period	Income-doubling Plan
1970–1980:	Shocks period	Nixon shock, oil shocks
1980–1990:	Internationalization period	Liberalization, trade surplus, capital export
1990–2000:	Trial period	Contributions to construction of the world order

of education of the Japanese nation in prewar and postwar Japan can be seen in Tables 15–19.

The percentage of junior high school graduates proceeding to high schools was almost 95 percent in 1989, and the percentage going to universities and junior colleges was 36.3 percent. This is comparable with the U.S. figure of 42 percent of the same age group enrolled in colleges and universities. Since, however, the U.S. figures include part-time students, the two figures may be interpreted as about the same. This educational parity was achieved around 1975, long before Japanese per capita GNP caught up with that of the United States.

Historically the Japanese government has devoted a very high portion of the government expenditure to education, since right after the Meiji Restoration. The number of primary schools increased from 12,597 in 1873 to 24,303 in 1875; that of middle schools from 20 to 116; and that of colleges from 26 to 110 in the same two years. But the government expenditure for education now is at about the same level as those in most Western countries, as Table 16 shows.

This does not mean that the expenditure in Japan is about the same as that in the United States per capita, because private schools are much more predominant, at least at higher education levels, in Japan than

TABLE 15   Numbers of Students in Japan

	National population (millions)	Level (thousands)						
		Primary	Middle	Girls'	Normal	College	Gymnasium	University
1873	35.1	1,326	1.8	—	—	4.1	—	—
1880	36.6	2,349	5.6	—	5.2	5.1	—	—
1890	39.9	3,096	11.6	3.1	5.3	10.3	4.4	1.3
1900	43.8	4,684	78.3	12.0	15.6	14.9	5.7	3.2
1910	49.1	6,862	122.3	56.2	25.4	33.0	6.3	7.2
1920	55.9	8,633	177.2	151.3	26.6	49.0	8.8	21.9
1930	64.4	10,112	345.7	369.0	43.9	90.0	20.6	69.6
1940	71.9	12,335	432.3	555.6	41.4	141.5	20.3	82.0
1945	72.1	12,818	639.8	875.8	56.3	213.0	21.7	98.8
1947	78.1	10,639	271.0	358.1	61.2	231.4	30.6	129.7

	National population (millions)	Level (thousands)					
		Jr. high	High school	Engineering college[a]	Jr. college	University	Others[b]
1950	83.2	5,332	1,935		15.1	224.9	503.4
1960	93.4	5,899	3,239		83.4	626.4	1,275.4
1970	103.7	4,716	4,231	44.3	263.2	1,406.5	1,403.5
1980	117.1	5,094	4,621	46.3	371.1	1,835.3	1,249.1
1989	122.6	5,619	5,645	52.0	461.8	2,066.9	1,280.5

Dash = not available.

a. The engineering colleges were started in 1965. The number here includes only those at the level of college: students in the last two years and also those in national schools for training engineering teachers.

b. Others include various vocational schools.

TABLE 16   Public Expenditure for Education as Percentage of National Income

	Japan	U.S.A.	U.K.	France	Germany	USSR
1961	4.6	6.9	4.5	3.0	5.1	7.1
1970	4.7	7.2	7.0	4.7	4.7	8.6
1975	6.5	7.6	8.2	5.0	6.4	9.0
1980	7.2	7.2	7.5	5.4	6.3	8.7
1983	7.1	7.3		6.0	6.4	8.2
1987	6.6					

in Europe or the United States. Table 17 shows the division between the private schools and the public (those run by national or local government) schools. The figures in percentage columns show the proportion of private schools among all levels of educational institutions in Japan. Clearly, except for the primary and junior high schools, which are compulsory in Japan, the private schools are predominant.

This does not mean that all the expenses of the private schools come completely from private sources. Approximately half of the expenses

TABLE 17   Public Schools vs. Private Schools in Japan, 1989

	School (thousands)	%	Students (thousands)	%	Teachers (thousands)	%
Kindergarten	15,080	58.3	2,037	77.4	100	75.0
Primary school	24,853	0.7	9,606	0.7	445	0.7
Middle school	11,264	5.4	5,619	3.5	286	3.2
High school	5,510	23.7	5,645	28.4	284	22.7
Engineering jr. college	62	6.5	52	5.7	4	4.4
Jr. college	584	83.9	462	90.1	20	82.5
University	499	72.9	2,067	72.6	121	50.8
graduate school	—	—	85	31.8	52	30.6
Other schools	7,761	82.3	1,197	92.7	42	76.1
Total	65,613	27.6	26,770	24.3	1,354	20.5

Dash = not available.

for teachers is subsidized by government, so that a fair amount of public expenditure for education actually goes to private educational institutions. Nevertheless, it is true that a significant portion of the expenditure for education has been borne by the private sector.

The domination of private schools, particularly at levels of higher education, seems to have had pros and cons. An advantage was that education could respond more quickly to the demand side, but a disadvantage was that the inexpensive fields of education were developed beyond the society's need for them. Examples of the former are the engineering departments, whereas examples of the latter are the easygoing liberal arts colleges, of which too many have been developed. (See Table 18.) On the whole the advantages seem to have dominated the disadvantages, as the system has responded very efficiently to social requirements by offering various kinds and levels of education to meet the education fervor among Japanese families and accommodate ever-growing industrial requirements.

The response to social needs seems to be more clearly observable at the graduate school levels. But the inflexibility of universities'

TABLE 18   Specialization of University Departments and Graduate Schools (percentage)

Field	Undergraduate		M.A. graduate studies		Ph.D. graduate studies	
	1978	1988	1978	1988	1978	1988
Humanities	13.3	14.7	15.3	10.5	15.8	13.0
Social sciences	41.2	39.1	12.6	9.5	13.8	9.8
Science	3.1	3.3	10.0	10.3	15.8	10.9
Engineering	19.7	19.8	42.6	45.1	15.2	14.1
Agronomy	3.4	3.4	7.7	8.4	6.3	5.7
Medical science	3.8	3.9	—	0.2	26.8	40.2
Pharmacy	2.0	2.0	3.0	3.7	2.2	2.1
Home economics	1.8	1.9				
Pedagogy	7.5	7.5	4.0	8.0	3.3	2.4
Others	4.2	4.4	4.8	4.4	0.8	1.0
Total	100.0	100.0	100.0	100.0	100.0	100.0

Blank cell = not applicable; dash = not available.

departmental composition seems to show different degrees of correspondence to social requirements, as can be seen in Table 19.

A more careful study is needed to see if the graduates are employed
in their proper specializations. The industries of their employers can
be found in the Fundamental Survey of Education. The improvement
of labor quality has been achieved by on- and off-the-job training within
private enterprises and government offices. The Japanese style of
management is based on lifetime employment, so that training and job
rotation are inseparable from the employment and management style.
This requires that enterprises themselves be solidly established and have
excellent management. In practice, the degrees of these conditions in
Japan are 86 percent for stable employment and 51.6 percent for job
rotation.[6] The quality of labor can be observed also in the morale of

TABLE 19   The Rate of Employment for Graduates (percentage)

| | College | | Junior college | |
Field	1978	1988	1978	1988
Humanities	57.1	74.5	68.7	82.7
Social sciences	77.4	86.1	71.4	80.4
Liberal arts			64.6	81.7
Sciences	63.3	69.2		
Engineering	82.4	81.0	77.4	80.9
Agronomy	69.4	78.0	72.0	66.9
Medical and health	44.1	42.5	84.2	82.5
medicine	2.7	1.1		
dentistry	66.1	48.2		
pharmacy	64.0	72.1		
other medical sciences	76.4	83.7		
Maritime	89.1	52.0		
Home economics	60.5	82.0	68.1	83.5
Pedagogy	73.5	68.9	78.3	85.2
Arts	49.4	64.1	49.0	61.3
Others	63.0	79.2	83.8	92.2
Total	71.9	77.8	71.0	82.0

Blank cell = not applicable.

workers in their jobs. This can be seen in the number of hours lost in one year; the rate of accidents; labor disputes; absenteeism; or, in general, the social crime rate. In all these aspects the Japanese rates are significantly lower than in most advanced economies.

Technological Progress

It is often said that Japan borrowed Western technology and improved it. The truth of this can be seen in the so-called technological balance of payments as shown in Table 20. There are two kinds of information making up these statistics: Bank of Japan data and Bureau of Statistics data in Japan. Table 21 shows that Japan is still far behind the United States in the technological balance but is already ahead of most European countries.

The expenditure for research and development (R&D) has increased very much in Japan as well as in many advanced countries, but that in Japan jumped in the 1970s and 1980s in comparison with other countries, as Table 22 shows.

In summary, one may observe that from 1966 to 1987 Japan's GNP increased 8.9 times, whereas R&D expenditure increased 18.4 times— the annual rate of increase is 14.8 percent—and the percentage from government funds increased 11.5 times. From 1970 to 1988 the number of researchers increased 2.6 times (the annual rate is 5.5 percent). With these remarkable increases in R&D expenditure and the number of researchers, one should certainly expect high returns resulting in an increase in technological innovations. Such results have shown up in the increase in patents obtained in Japan and abroad. From 1966 to 1987 the patents applied for in Japan increased from 62,962 to 311,006—5 times. The patents granted increased 3.1 times.

The Japanese effort in improving technology can be seen in its rapid increase in R&D expenditure and the number of researchers in the 1970s and the 1980s. R&D expenditure in 1970 was only 1,195 million (about 11.59 billion) yen but that in 1987 was 9,016 million (about 90.16 billion) yen, so that the annual rate of increase was 12.6 percent. The number of R&D personnel in 1970 was 392 thousand, and that in 1988 was 715 thousand, so that the annual rate of increase was 3.4 percent. But the

TABLE 20 Japan's Technological Balance of Payments

	Bank of Japan			Bureau of Statistics			
	Receipts (millions of dollars)	Payments (millions of dollars)	Ratio (%)	Receipts (billions of yen)		Payments (billions of yen)		Ratio (%)
1966	17	192	0.09						
1971	60	488	0.12	27.2	(11.1)	134.5	(15.6)	0.20	(0.71)
1980	376	1,439	0.26	159.6	(74.3)	239.5	(27.7)	0.66	(2.68)
1987	1,385	4,177	0.33	215.6	(44.8)	283.2	(56.2)	0.76	(0.79)

NOTE: The figures in parentheses in Bureau of Statistics data are those for new contracts.

TABLE 21 Technological Balance of Payments of Major Countries, 1975–1987 (millions of U.S. dollars)

	Japan	U.S.A.	U.K.	Germany	France	Italy
1975						
Receipts	233	4,008	589	264	394	90
Payments	592	473	578	679	472	480
Ratio (%)	0.39	8.47	1.02	0.39	0.83	0.19
1980						
Receipts	644	6,617	779	430	688	233
Payments	966	762	672	1,025	823	662
Ratio (%)	0.67	8.68	1.16	0.42	0.83	0.35
1985						
Receipts	982	16,669	848	614	894	144
Payments	1,229	6,215	692	1,206	1,064	546
Ratio (%)	0.80	2.68	1.22	0.51	0.84	0.26
1987						
Receipts	1,490	22,281	980	1,081	1,348	301
Payments	1,958	8,877	908	2,443	1,732	788
Ratio (%)	0.76	2.51	1.08	0.44	0.78	0.38

number of researchers increased from 172 thousand in 1970 to 442 thousand in 1988, the annual rate of increase being 5.4 percent.

These increases correspond to the rapid growth of the Japanese economy and its gains in a competitive edge in international trade after the oil shocks. This can be seen by observing the correspondence between the export industries and their R&D expenditure and number of researchers. The list of industries in Table 23 shows the ratios of R&D expenditures to net sales in major industries in 1987 and the number of researchers in these industries, in 1981 and 1988.

Notice in Table 23 that the small and medium-sized enterprises still make up an important portion of Japanese industries even now, and their R&D expenditures are also fairly significant. Even small enterprises are spending nearly 2 percent of their net sales for R&D. But the number of researchers is much greater in large corporations. The concentration of researchers in large corporations is very significant; nevertheless, the concentration ratios differ greatly from one industry to another.

TABLE 22   Research and Development Expenditure in Selected Countries

	Japan	U.S.A.	USSR	Germany	France	U.K.
1975 expenditure ($ billions)	15.5					
% of national income	2.1					
% from public funds	27.5					
1980 expenditure ($ billions)	27.8	62.6				
% of national income	2.4	2.6				
% from public funds	25.8	47.1				
1985 expenditure ($ billions)	48.2	107.4				
% of national income	3.2	3.0				
% from public funds	19.4	47.7				
1987 expenditure ($ billions)	62.3	118.7	43.1[a]	31.6	20.5	12.9[a]
% of national income	3.3	3.3	5.0	3.1	2.6	2.7
% from public funds	19.9	48.2	48.3	37.7	43.7	38.5

Blank cell = not applicable.
a. USSR and UK figures are for 1986. The 1986 figures for Korea are 1,523 billion won (about 1.5 trillion), which is 2.3% of national income and of which 19.0% came from government funds.

TABLE 23 Japanese Industrial Effort in Research and Development, 1981 and 1988

	Net sales (billions of yen)	R&D ratio (%)	Researchers (thousands) 1981	Researchers (thousands) 1988
All industries	2,503	2.59	185.0	279.0
Employee size 1–299, capital size ¥10 million	232	1.75	2.0	2.0
Employee size 300–999, capital size ¥10–100 million	317	1.76	21.0	24.0
Employee size 1,000–2,999, capital size ¥100 million–1 billion	469	1.95	31.0	33.0
Employee size 3,000–9,999, capital size ¥1 billion–10 billion	624	2.40	48.0	61.0
Employee size 10,000 and above, capital size ¥10 billion and above	859	3.61	80.0	159.0
Special institutions			3.0	0.4
Agriculture, forestry, fishing	19	0.31	0.3	0.2
Mining	16	1.01	0.6	0.7
Construction	248	0.51	5.0	6.0
Manufacturing	1,944	3.14	175.0	267.0
Food processing	180	0.99	8.0	10.0
Textiles	46	1.42	2.0	4.0
Paper pulp	43	0.77	1.0	2.0
Publishing, printing	27	0.80	0.5	1.0

Chemistry	241	4.53	32.0	47.0
Petroleum products	109	0.64	2.0	2.0
Plastics	39	2.16	—	4.0
Rubber products	26	3.25	3.0	4.0
Ceramics	63	2.82	5.0	7.0
Iron and steel	102	2.40	5.0	6.0
Nonferrous metals	54	1.90	3.0	4.0
Metal products	63	1.50	4.0	6.0
General machinery	140	2.99	15.0	23.0
Electrical machinery	385	5.61	59.0	104.0
Transportation machinery	301	3.22	18.0	26.0
Precision machinery	41	4.91	7.0	21.0
Others	76	1.12	8.0	6.0
Transportation, commerce, public utilities	274	0.84	4.0	4.0

Blank cell = not applicable.

The Role of Government

The predominant portion of Japanese R&D was undertaken by private industries, but the Japanese government played an essential role in promoting some frontiers of industrial research. The Council for Science and Technology was placed directly under the prime minister. The Japanese government's general guideline for science and technology is clearly stated in the cabinet decision made on March 28, 1986, "General Guideline for Science and Technology Policy." This is really a continuation and restatement of the policies already being more or less pursued by the government throughout the postwar years.

The "General Guideline" says that "highly creative science and technology should be the core of the nation's science and technology policy if we are to respond correctly to our various needs, to make our society and national life richer in the coming twenty-first century as well as to open up new possibilities in the future. . . . In encouraging creative science and technology, it is important to develop and strengthen favorable systems and conditions for R&D activities." The document states the priority programs as follows:

1. developing and strengthening systems for science and technology

2. developing and improving conditions for R&D

   • increasing R&D investment

   • securing and training R&D personnel

   • consolidating the basis for science and technology promotion

   • expanding international exchange and cooperation in science and technology

   • promoting public understanding and securing cooperation

3. Encouraging important areas of research and development

   • encouraging basic, leading sciences and technologies in which new progress can be expected

- encouraging sciences and technologies for activating the economy

- encouraging sciences and technologies for improving the quality of society and life

The government allocated its budget according to these principles and tried to promote R&D along these lines in the government's own research institutes and national universities, of which there are many.

NOTES

1. These factors are discussed in "The Pattern and Process of Asian Economic Development," in *The Challenge of Asian Economic Development,* edited by S. Ichimura (Tokyo: Asian Productivity Organization, 1988).

2. The interested reader with a knowledge of Japanese should read the following books: Hiroya Ueno, *Industrial Policy in Japan* (in Japanese) (Tokyo: Nihon Keizai: Shinbun-sha, 1987), and Ryutaro Komiya, ed., *Nihonno Sangyo Seisaku* (Japanese industrial policy) (Tokyo: University of Tokyo Press, 1984). Brief expositions are given in my English working papers *Japanese Industrial Restructuring Policies* (Discussion Paper, Center for Southeast Asian Studies, 1980) and *Moving up the Market* (Discussion Paper, Center for Southeast Asian Studies, Kyoto University, 1982).

3. One should not take this fact as something that automatically accompanies economic growth in any country. For instance, in the case of Latin American countries these ratios have not increased with the rise in per capita income; in some countries the saving ratios have stabilized at around 20 percent, and in some countries they are coming down. Among the Asian–Pacific countries of our sample only the Philippines shows a saving behavior similar to that of Latin America. Except for Singapore and Taiwan, household saving rates for our sample reach a ceiling slightly below 30 percent regardless of per capita income level. Significant though this is for the relative success of the growth strategies for all these countries, the effect of the disparities in per capita income level among our four types of economies is clearly reflected in the resource gap each has characteristically experienced and consequently in the extent to which each has had to borrow from abroad to sustain its rate of capital accumulation and growth in the recent past.

4. ICOR is important, because the ratio of capital formation to GDP divided by ICOR determines the growth rate of GDP.

5. See Karl Deutsch, "Social Mobilization and Political Development," *American Political Science Review,* September 1961; Samuel P. Huntington, *Political Order in Changing Societies* (New Haven, Conn.: Yale University Press, 1968); Myron Weiner and S. P. Huntington, eds., *Understanding Political Development* (Boston: Little, Brown, 1987).

6. The interested reader may refer back to the first essay in this monograph. The so-called Japanese-style management is practiced in bigger corporations more widely than in small and medium-sized enterprises, and the difference is significant among individual enterprises.